CHANGE DIRECTIONS

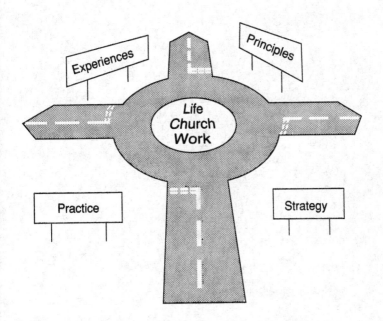

By the same author:

Seconds Away!
Team Spirit
Peacing Together
A Guide to Total Quality Management

Change Directions

New ways forward for your life,
your church and your business

DAVID CORMACK

MONARCH
Crowborough

British Library Cataloguing in Publication Data
A catalogue record for this book is available
from the British Library.

ISBN: 1 85424 310 1

Designed and produced by Bookprint Creative Services
P.O. Box 827, BN21 3YJ, England for
MONARCH PUBLICATIONS
Broadway House, The Broadway
Crowborough, East Sussex, TN6 1HQ.
Printed in Finland by WSOY

CONTENTS

To
Mother
for her first ninety years
in a changing world

ACKNOWLEDGEMENTS

This book owes its contents to all those friends, colleagues and acquaintances who have helped me learn about life and living. They, or their marks, appear in every chapter – my thanks and my apologies to them all.

Change Directions contains a number of real examples of radical change in churches, missions and organisations. I am grateful to all those individuals and organisations whose permission was needed to prepare this book. Some of the contributions are anonymous in order to protect the confidentiality of those involved, others are listed in the text.

Change Directions went off the road a number of times during its early life: it owes its existence to the computer skills of Cameron, without his ingenuity at retrieval several crashes would have been the end!

I would like to recognise the influence of Bryn Hughes whose studies in change management at Oxford and whose enthusiasm for learning has led to significant changes in this text – and in my life.

Finally I must mention Andrew Freemantle, the Chief Executive of the Scottish Ambulance Service for his outstanding example of leadership in change.

INTRODUCTION

Change is a common but complex topic. To help you come to grips with it *Change Directions* is set out in three parts. The first part deals with the principles of change, the second part deals with the practice of change and the final part deals with the experiences of change. The three parts are set out diagrammatically below. Each chapter follows the patterns shown in the wheels. I trust that these diagrams will help you find your way around a subject which is as complex as life itself – and that is because life is about change.

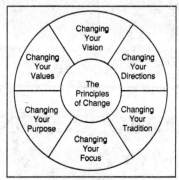

Part one: The Principles of Change

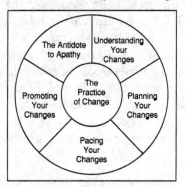

Part Two: The Practice of Change

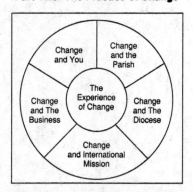

Part Three: The Experience of Change

PART ONE

The Principles of Change

CHAPTER ONE

CHANGING YOUR DIRECTION

I am making everything new.[1]

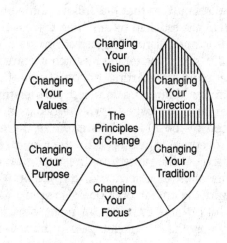

Culture is the way we do things and our generation has changed the way we do things more than any other in history. Welcome to the culture revolution! Wherever you look there has been change of unprecedented magnitude. Radical and revolutionary changes have made dramatic impacts on all levels of our society.

13

Turbulent World

The dramatic changes which swept through Eastern Europe and the Soviet Union at the beginning of the 1990s left many people, including governments, stunned, overwhelmed and unable to grasp the significance of the events or to cope with their consequences. Assumptions, beliefs and prejudices were swept aside in the white water of unanticipated social revolution. These unpredictable changes were not confined to the old communist world of the early 1990s. Wherever you lived on planet Earth in those days you were caught up in your own revolution of change.

The sexual revolution that has followed the onslaught of HIV and AIDS has touched us all. Then there is the fact that nationally, this and all future generations will live downstream of the social watershed which occured in 1994, when more children starting school came from single parent situations than from married partnerships. At the international level the tragedies of the Lebanon and Timor were replaced by Bosnia and Rwanda as these countries attempted to come to terms with their own agonies of transformation. At the same time the ecological and environmental disasters of Chernobyl, the Exxon Valdez, the Gulf War and the threat of global warming focused the world's attention and priorities in new ways. Every day and in every way the rate of change continues to accelerate.

The trouble for most of us is not that one life-shaking trauma is threatening to overturn our little world; the problem is that changes small, many, frequent and all-pervading are transforming our familiar reference points and creating an alien landscape. We are faced with the crisis of ten thousand changes.

The cumulative effect of these changes confronts us daily. Changes in morality and living patterns have all but destroyed the family base for the majority in our society. Technical and economic changes are transforming the way so many of us live and work. Then of course there are the changes in the Church.

The Church, that last great bastion of tradition and stability, that last still point in a turbulent world is still no more. In 1964 the Catholic Church abolished the Latin Mass. In 1974 it became possible for divorced people to be remarried in some churches. In 1984 unions between partners of the same sex were being consecrated in churches and in 1994 the Church of England ordained its first woman priests. Some, finding these and the many smaller changes hurtful, threatening or simply unacceptable started to look for more stable traditions and found them in traditions which pre-date the Christian era.

Now, everywhere we look we see the signs, symbols and consequences of change – and most of it disturbs us because most of it seems to be change for the worse. Even those changes which we see as being for the better seem to be happening too fast for comfort or too slow to be of encouragement. We don't want to stop the world, but could some parts go a little slower and some parts a little faster please?

Unnerving

As I list all these changes, I recall an unnerving experience some years ago in the Scottish mountains when, without warning, a blizzard hit our hill walking group. One moment we were pushing up toward a mountain pass between two peaks, the next we were totally disoriented in a swirling, snowy white-out. We could not see where we were going nor where we had come from. We could not go back. We could not go forward. All we could do was dig in and wait for the storm to pass. I can still recall the fear of being totally disoriented and without reference points. Compass and map are useless when you cannot see where you are or where you want to go. The feeling of disorientation and helplessness was complete. Confusion is often the first consequence of unexpected change. The second consequence is an urgent and desperate search for certainty and security.

The response of many people to the confusing transformations in today's world has been similar to my own on that directionless mountainside – dig in and wait for better times! The trouble with this strategy is that if you wait too long, you die to reality, unable to cope with life as you find it; you chose to live out of touch with a world that is too painful to live in.

An alternative response is to face the world and its changes and to take the steps that you must take in order to survive, even though you find the steps threatening. You cannot live your life insulated from the world and its changes. We are children of our times and our times are times of change.

There is a third response open to us all – to recognise that although change is inevitable, it is not predictable or predetermined. Change itself is open to change; it is open to influence. We can learn not only to master the change process, but we can learn to be agents of change, shaping its form and direction. The choice is ours.

Survival

Those who do not learn to change die before their time. As one commentator put it, 'The gulf between how one should live and how one does live is so wide that a man who neglects what is actually done for what should be done learns the way to self-destruction rather than self-preservation.'[2] This statement from the sixteenth century is as true today as it was then. Ask the miner whose pit and community are no more; ask the worshipper whose church is now a mosque, warehouse or holiday home; ask the family

– so called – split apart by selfishness or intolerance. Change is neccessary for survival. There is no longer a place in a changing world for those who cannot or will not change. The present and the future belong to the pioneers, to the pilgrims, to the pupils and students of change and to all those who are prepared to learn to change. The meek shall inherit the earth, but I believe this will only be because they are humble enough to learn what it takes to be around when everyone else has died from terminal inflexibility!

In the closing hours of the 1980s, the world looked on amazed as the rigid regimes of the Eastern Bloc countries in Europe were swept away by the forces of irresistible change. The fixed old guard could not change, could not adapt, could not bend and therefore was broken. The changes were neither easy nor painless, nor were there available counsellors skilled in the process of transition and transformation. No person, organisation or society was equipped to withstand the cyclone of change which hit our unsuspecting generation – none that is except the Church.

The God of Change

Change is the Church's business. It is the Church's business because change is God's business. The Bible reveals a master plan for change – personal, relational, social and universal. Change is God's agenda.

'I am the First and the Last . . . who was, and is, and is to come';[3] 'I the Lord do not change';[4] '. . . from everlasting to everlasting you are God'.[5] Such are the revelations of the unchanging God, the Yahweh of the Bible, in contrast with today's flexible but all too fragile world in constant transition. We change.

Yet the God of Jesus, the immutable God of the Christians is also revealed as the God of all change. He is the creator God who transforms darkness into light. He is the liberating God who transforms a million slaves into a nation of priest-led warriors. He is the God of resurrection who changes death into life. He is the God of reconciliation who changes disintegration into integration. He is the God of eternity whose pleasure it is to continually make all things new.

This changeless but transforming Deity calls us into a living relationship with Himself and that living relationship calls for change. The One who does not change is in the business of change and requires that the Church as a body and its members as individuals be partners with Him in the process of world, societal and personal transformation.

The People of Change

Encounters with the changeless God result in fundamental and profound personal changes. 'Conversion' is almost too weak a word to describe the experiences of people such as Isaiah,[6] Ezekiel,[7] Zechariah the father of John the Baptist, Mary the mother of Jesus,[9] St Paul[10] and St John the Divine.[11] For them the encounters caused despair, fear, trauma, awe and wonder. Yet the truth is that this awesome transforming power of God is experienced by all those who enter into that living relationship in Christ. If anyone is in Christ, he is a new creation; the old has gone, the new has come![12] This is hardly the description of a marginal change, for at the heart of the Christian experience and message is reconciliation – a 'thorough changing' of relationships.[13]

But the coming of the new life is not a one-off experience. Faith is pilgrimage – a process of continuous change, for the Bible knows nothing about a static relationship with God. God expects change and encourages His people to seek change.

The Scriptures give many examples of prayer and

change. There is prayer for change in personal condition: Hannah prayed for a son and 'the Lord remembered her.'[14] There is prayer for change in the condition of others: Elisha prays for the dead son of the Shunammite.[15] There is prayer for the spiritual condition of the family as Job prayed for his children.[16] There is prayer for the spiritual condition of the nation.[17] This same tradition of praying for change is extended into the New Testament, where, following Christ's examples Saint Paul prays for himself,[18] his friends,[19] churches[20] and the Jewish nation.[21]

Prayer has many functions. It is worship, it is communion, it is praise, it is thanksgiving, it is intercession, it is confession, it is repentance and it is meditation. But first and foremost, prayer is opening ourselves to the God who is able to change us. When we open ourselves to the God of change then we open ourselves to change. If we pray for change then the first result we need to be prepared for is a change in ourselves.

The Ministry of Change

To be in communion with the God of change, to experience His power to change and to be His witnesses as salt and light in our society means that change must be a hallmark of our personal life as Christians. Change must also be a core tradition of our corporate life as the Church, the Body of Christ. Change is thus an integral part of our ministry to a world which does not need less change but rather needs more change.

I believe that the Church's role in relation to change is four-fold:

1. To continually renew itself;
2. To provide an environment for personal and spiritual change and growth;

3. To call for change and be leaders of change in our society;
4. To minister to a society which is collapsing under the burden of unmanaged and destructive change.

In this book I want to describe the skills, techniques and the experiences of Christians who are rediscovering the God of all change. I want to describe the lessons that are emerging from Christians as they attempt to transform their churches, missions and businesses and to minister to a world which is in a state of terminal change. The content of *Change Directions* will thus enable the readers to:

1. Gain insight into change as God's tool for personal, corporate and social transformation;
2. Understand the techniques of change management and how to use it;
3. Apply the principles and practices of change management to their own lives, situations, churches, organisations and societies.

The text contains a number of exercises which you are encouraged to complete as you encounter them. In addition there are a number of examples of the various principles and practices described. These case studies are included in Part Three for those who would seek a deeper understanding of change and the Church, mission or organisation.

The Change Conspiracy

Change is God's way of restoring creation to Himself. The Church is called to use the ministry of change in its own pilgrimage and to demonstrate to society the power and willingness of God to transform each and every aspect of His creation. But, somewhere along the road to the third millennium, change got a bad name. Maybe it was in that first garden when the first change on offer was the knowledge of evil. Maybe it was when the Church Fathers established traditions and creeds in various attempts to guide the faithful and keep them on the straight and narrow path. Maybe it was the result of the Reformation when fear, suspicion and defensiveness resulted in a fixing of positions and a closing of minds. Maybe it came with the so-called Age of Reason when knowledge became a destination rather than a point of departure. Maybe it was the impact of the destructive moral liberalism which swept through most of the developed world in the second half of the twentieth century. Probably it was all of these and more. Whatever the roots, change became bad news for the Church. Consequently the people of God have become less able to fulfil their four-fold ministry of change either corporately or personally. For too many Christians their pilgrimage has become one long struggle against change rather than a welcoming embracing of the Lord of change.

The counter-change conspiracy is anti-Christian in origin. Christians are the people of transformation not conformation. Our real challenge is not to hold some imaginary theological line, or even go back to some old traditional position. Our real challenge is to go forward as leaders and learners and to embrace the transforming power of God which is our unique heritage.

The World of Change

It is relatively easy to illustrate the Church's aversion to change. Consider your own world for a moment. In Table 1.1, Column A, make a list of the major changes that you have seen in society in the last twenty five years.

Now make a list of the major changes which have taken place in your own church over the last twenty years. List them in Column B. A comparison of Columns A and B will illustrate the lack of relevant change within the Church

	Column A *Major changes in society*	Column B *Major changes in my church*
1		
2		
3		
4		
5		
6		
7		
8		
9		
10		

Table 1.1. *Changes in the past twenty-five years*

generally. Most people will not be able to list more than five in Column B. How did you do?

During the 1980s as Director of Management Training for MARC Europe, a Christian development organisation, I conducted a large number of seminars for Christian leaders of many nationalities on the subject of change. During the course of these seminars I asked the delegates to make a list of changes that they felt the Church needed to make if it was to fully respond to the challenges and opportunities of the times. Table 1.2 shows the changes these leaders thought were most needed.

It will be clear from your own answers in Table 1.1 that the Church in the second half of the twentieth century fell far behind society in its rate of change. The Church lost its role as the promoter and champion of change. Both radical and continuous change became the tools of government and business while the Church struggled to maintain its own status quo and became increasingly allergic to change.

	The Change required by the Church
1	To have a restored voice in national affairs.
2	To have a new vision for those outside the Church.
3	To recognise and utilise women's gifts.
4	To have more effective leadership.
5	To take socially relevant initiatives.
6	To overcome historical architectural building constraints.
7	To learn to use the media effectively.
8	To have Godly planning and management.
9	To have more realistic financial support.
10	To have a committed membership.

Table 1.2. *Most needed changes in the Church*

This was not always the case. It is interesting to contrast today's Church with the Church down through the ages.

The Jesus of the Gospels was a bringer of change. No one spoke like Him. No one interpreted the law like Him. His behaviour shocked the traditionally established norms of the religious leaders of His generation. Within twenty-five years of His crucifixion, the early Church, with all its radical teaching, was transforming lives, businesses and communities and was beginning to emerge as a threat to the basic values of an increasingly corrupt Roman Empire.

Although there have been periods of quiescence, stagnation and repression of change in the life of the Church, it was the Church which, to a large extent, fostered the Renaissance, the Reformation and the Industrial Revolution. With the rise of industrial economies in the nineteenth century, it was often the Christian employers who pioneered the social changes relating to education and family welfare.

In the nineteenth and twentieth centuries, the Christian

vision for mission transformed Christianity from a first world religion to a universal Church. Of course things were changing in the Church too. Pressures from without and within were giving rise to conflict, division and fragmentation. Throughout the twentieth century, the numbers of church attenders have been declining in the traditional bastions of the faith in the developed world. Change was becoming a liability rather than a responsibility in a Church which saw its future increasingly in its past. But these generalisations are not true of all churches, denominations or individuals. Renewal has continued in some traditions and is reappearing in others. It is from these that the Church must learn if it is to regain its lost heritage as the agent of the God of change in a changing world. The Church must learn again to change the way it does things. It is time to change our culture radically. Our God is not finished with us yet.

Challenge

John Stott in his book *Issues Facing Christians Today* identifies five challenges for the Church. These were to:

1. Be children of your Father;
2. Create and share your vision;
3. Work to realise the vision;
4. Persevere, endure, don't accept second best;
5. Serve those whom you seek to help.[22]

I would like to add another one, perhaps even more fundamental than these five, for without it the five will not be realised.

6. The greatest challenge facing the Church today is the need to see that change is God's way forward.

This text will help you understand change, it will help you cope with change, it will help you manage change, but if that is all that it does it will have failed in its main purpose. The purpose of *Change Directions* is that Christians – individually and in community – might regain their inheritance as God's agents of change. Are you ready to begin to work to change the direction in which your life, your church and your business has been heading? Good! But before you begin Chapter Two, reflect on these study points for your own church, mission or organisation.

Reflections on Changing Your Direction

1. When was the last time we initiated a radical change in the way we do things?

   ....

2. What one thing would we like to change but at the moment cannot see a way of making the change?

   ....

3. What things are no longer a strong feature of our church or organisation which we regret losing?

   ....

   ....

4. What is causing us to lose touch with our 'customers' in our market place?

   ....

   ....

5. What has our church done to respond to the ten changes listed in Table 1.2. page 23?

   ....

   ....

References in Chapter One

1. Revelation 21:5.
2. Machiavelli Niccolo, *The Prince*, Penguin Classics, Penguin Books, 1984, p. 91.
3. Revelation 1:17 and 4:8.
4. Malachi 3:6.
5. Psalm 90:2.
6. Isaiah 6:5.
7. Ezekiel 2:15.
8. St. Luke 1:12.
9. St Luke 1:29.
10. Acts 9:9.
11. Revelation 1:17.
12. 2 Corinthians 5:17.
13. Cormack, David, *Peacing Together*, Monarch Publications, 1989.
14. 1 Samuel 1:19.
15. 2 Kings 4:5.
16. Job 1:5.
17. Numbers 21:7.
18. 2 Corinthians 12:8.
19. 2 Timothy 1:3.
20. 1 Thessalonians 1:2.
21. Romans 10:1.
22. Stott, John, *Issues Facing Christians Today*, Chapter 17, pp. 327–339, Marshall Morgan and Scott, 1984.

CHAPTER TWO

CHANGING YOUR TRADITION

You have heard it was said 'Love your neighbour and hate your enemy'. But I say unto you: Love your enemies and pray for those that persecute you, that you may be sons of your Father in heaven.[1]

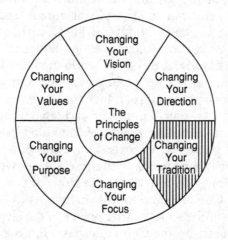

'The church is always in need of renewal'[2]. So said the contributors to Vatican II, that great watershed review of the Roman Catholic Church in 1963. That document set out a new agenda for Catholics worldwide. At its core were five basic initiatives designed to change the Church for the twenty-first century:[3]

27

1. The renewal of the whole Church, clergy and laity;
2. The evangelisation of those on the fringes of the Church;
3. The creation of faith-sharing communities;
4. The experiencing of salvation in the every day of life;
5. The rediscovery of the value of the traditions of the Church.

It is over 30 years since this agenda was set out and some would say that very little has been accomplished in that time. Yet change there certainly has been.

Power to Change

It is clear that the greater the historical tradition of an organisation, mission or church, the longer change will take to occur. In the early days of the Church, in the first and second centuries, change was the hallmark of Christianity. Christianity turned the world upside down. No aspect of life, society or culture was left untouched by the radicalness of the Gospel. In Acts 16 we see the very basis of business, social, domestic and legal systems challenged by the liberating power of the Good News.[4] The Gospel has power to change. However, power of this nature is threatening not only to those with power outside the Church, but also to those in positions of power within the Church. One response to this threat was to attempt to limit the use of the supernatural power of the Gospel; laws were introduced by the Church leaders, limits prescribed and controls imposed – in a word 'traditions' emerged.

In the independent states of the old USSR, the new religious freedom has given rise to the proliferation of churches, most of which reflect the fragmentation of Western faith. But each day the Russian Orthodox Church is growing in power and influence. For the Russian Orthodox Church the traditions of the Fathers, together with the Scriptures are the foundations of faith. It regards the 'new' Christianity of the West as suspect since the post-Reformation faiths do not put the traditions of the Fathers on a par with Scripture. As one Orthodox writer states:

> Belief in the holiness, divine inspiration, inviolability and universal obligatory character of the Tradition, on a par with the Scriptures, is one of the basic features of the One Holy Catholic Apostolic Church of Christ.[5]

On a recent visit to Armenia I spent time with the leaders of the Armenian Apostolic Church which regards even the Orthodox churches as being heretical! This was bad news for a post-Reformation, non-conformist like myself whose traditions are minimal and of recent origin.

It is the controlling nature of tradition which constrains change or inhibits it completely. Tradition is a safeguard, but it can also be a dangerous gaoler. But do we really need to protect ourselves from the power of God and its ablity to change us?

Charities

So too for the charity sector – tradition can become a trap. The origins of modern charity work are in philanthropic benevolence – the giving of those who have to those who have not. This is a fundamental feature of all truly mature societies. As one French scientist expressed it:

> I have the weakness to believe that it is an honour for a society to desire the expensive luxury of sustaining life for its useless, incompetent, and incurably ill members. I would almost measure society's degree of civilization by the amount of effort and vigilance it imposes on itself out of pure respect for life. It is noble to struggle unrelentingly to save someone's life as if he were dear to us, when objectively he has no value and is not even loved by anyone.[6]

However charity is too important to be left to government or the individual. Charity must be by the people for the people. Charity is big business not only in size but in social

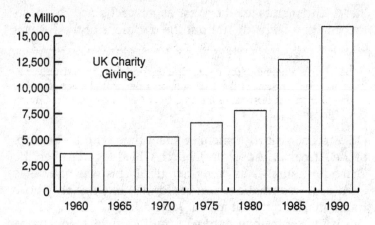

Figure 2.1. *UK charity giving*

importance. Where church attendance has declined in Western Europe in the second half of the twentieth century, charity involvement has increased. Figure 2.1 shows the level of charity giving in the UK over the last 30 years.[7]

The management of such sums and the management of the increasing number of full-time, part-time and volunteer workers is no mean task and has given rise to a new breed of charity professionals, people to whom charity is not only (or even) a means of expressing love for their neighbour but a means to a salary, a livelihood and a career.

The arrival of the sophisticated, professionally managed charity or mission has meant that many traditional charities have lost income and have had to radically change to survive or have simply closed their doors for lack of support. Many are still in the throes of transition and many will fail in the years ahead because they are unable to change quickly enough in the face of rapidly growing social needs and rapidly changing fund-raising methods.

Attitudes to Change Questionnaire

How much does tradition constrain you? Let us look briefly at your own attitudes to change. Complete the following short self-assessment questionnaire.

Each of the following four sets of five statements relate to change. Score each statement out of 5 according to your attitude to change. Thus a statement which is very like you is scored 5 and a statement which is totally opposite to your view is scored 0.

Score 5: Very like my attitude or view.
Score 4: Generally like my attitude or view.
Score 3: Somewhat like my attitude or view.
Score 2: Rarely like my attitude or view.
Score 1: Very unlike my attitude or view.
Score 0: Totally opposite to my view.

Statements Set A

1. I dislike change. ☐

2. Change is inevitable, but needs to be introduced slowly. ☐

3. There are good features and bad features in most changes. ☐

4. Change is essential for progress. ☐

5. Life is about change. ☐

Statements Set B

1. I think things are not as good as they used to be. ☐

2. I am happy to see things change one step at a time. ☐

3. With change I believe you cannot please all the people all the time, but you should at least try. ☐

4. Change is inevitable so we should learn to make the most of it. ☐

5. If necessary I would impose change on others if I felt it was for their own good. ☐

Statements Set C

1. I like to go back to the same place for my holidays. ☐

2. Better the devil you know than the devil you do not know. ☐

3. The priority in change should be to carry people with you. ☐

4. I am prepared to push for change, even when I know people are against it. ☐

5. I believe in getting change in place as quickly as possible. ☐

Statements Set D

1. I dislike uncertainty. ☐

2. I am careful not to throw the baby out with the bath water. ☐

3. Most people will accept change if you give them time to understand it. ☐

4. I am always keen to try something new. ☐

5. Revolutions are necessary to achieve some changes. ☐

Now take your scores and place them in Table 2.1 and read on to determine their significance.

Set	Scores from Statement Number				
	1	2	3	4	5
A					
B					
C					
D					
Totals					

Table 2.1. *Self-assessment scores for attitude to change*

Extremes

We all view change differently. Our attitudes often depend on what change means for us, is it good for us or is it bad for us? Niccolo Machiavelli, observing the world of six-teenth century Italy, commented that those who benefited from change were the most supportive of that change, but those who benefited from the way things were, often posed the strongest opposition to change. A further observation was that the support of those who would benefit from the change was less obvious than the opposition from those who benefited from the status quo.[8] Although written over four hundred years ago, Machiavelli could have been prophesying the events in Russia at the end of the twentieth century.

But is not simply the benefits or disadvantages of a change that influence our attitudes towards it. More impor-tant in determining our views of change are our values and beliefs. What is important to us? How do we view the world? How do we view our knowledge? For some people knowledge is finite, what they have learned is all there is to learn; what they know is all that there is to know. The position they hold is the only right position – for such people change is bad, evil, regressive and to be avoided at all costs. If your current values, beliefs and knowledge are considered correct, then any movement is a movement away from the truth as you see it.

At the opposite end of the spectrum are the people who believe that all knowledge is relative, there are no absolute truths, there is nothing that is worthy of preserving or maintaining – only what exists or is possible is right. For such people change is good and desirable.

We could caricature these two extreme positions as the Traditionalist and the Radical – the first attempting to hold on to the past as long as possible, the latter attempting to overthrow the present as quickly as possible. The state of change is like a besieged city – those inside the change want out and those outside the change want in! As Macaulay describes the army faced with stiff resistance:

Those behind cried 'Forward' and those before cried 'Back'![9]

In between there are two other sets of values – those of the Conservative who would like to change only a few features of the world, and those of the Progressive who is interested in seeing considerable change but not in every area; some things, but not a lot are worth keeping. Figure 2.2 illustrates the types.

Of the four attitudes, the Radical is the most willing to change but even the Radical has limits and will resist some changes. In the same way the Traditionalist, although generally resistant to change, will accept some change. So, both the Radical and the Traditionalist have their absolutes – those things to which they hold unswervingly.

It is neither good nor bad to be Radical, Progressive, Conservative or Traditional. They are simply different. However, when you seek to introduce change you must understand the attitudes of the people that you are asking to change. In all groups you will find a mix of attitudes. Whether you are dealing with a family, a church, a busi-

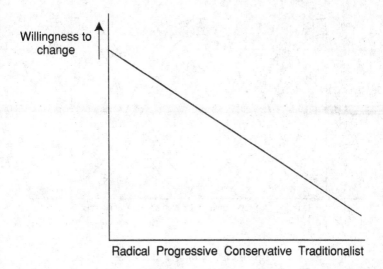

Radical Progressive Conservative Traditionalist

Figure 2.2. *Attitudes to change*

ness or a political party there are always the four attitudes represented. Even the most radical of groups have their traditionalists who want their revolutions to be done in the good old traditional manner! While those groups dedicated to yesterday also have their radicals who want to move the clock forward a nanosecond or two!

Figure 2.3 shows the typical distribution of the four types in any organisation. Most of the people are either Progressive or Conservative in attitude. Traditionalists and Radicals are invariably in the minority. The trouble is that the noise that these two minorities make is often in inverse proportion to their numbers. The fewer they are the more voluble they seem to become! The danger is that the leader listens to the minority rather than main population.

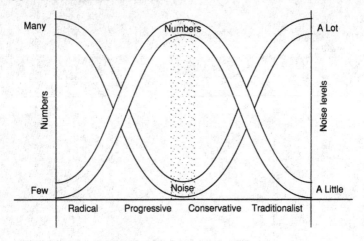

Figure 2.3. *Numbers and noise*

The Silent Minority

There is of course a fifth attitude to change – the Progressive Conservative or the Conservative Progressive. These are the people of the centre ground. They are the silent minority represented by the dotted area of Figure 2.3. Silent they may be but they are not without influence. They are the opinion-formers of society. They are the reference points used by everyone – Radicals, Progressives, Conservatives and Traditionalists alike. People listen to them. People respect them. They are the people of real power.

When you seek to introduce change it is vital that you gain the support of this silent minority. They are the passive persuaders, the 'midwives of change'. They must not be overlooked. Win their hearts and minds and your task of implementing change will be greatly facilitated. Table 2.2 shows the main features of the five types. Can you recognise your usual response to change?

Type description	Typical attitudes
1. The Radical attitude	Loves to pioneer new initiatives. All change is wonderfully exciting. Nothing is good around here. Everything has to change and has to change fast and I'm the one to do it! Traditionalists are reactionaries.
2. The Progressive attitude	Likes the pioneer, but prefers a slower rate of change. Most change is exciting as long as there is not too much risk. Not everything needs to change, but most does.
3. The Conservative attitude	Suspicious of the radical pioneer. Most change is somewhat threatening. Most things are OK around here. A little fine-tuning here and there never did anyone any harm.
4. The Traditional attitude	Radicals are revolutionaries and hence very dangerous. All change is very threatening. Things are OK here apart from what has been changed recently. Let us go back to the good old days.
5. The Progressive Conservative or the Conservative Progressive attitude	Change is necessary, but people view change differently. Traditionalists need to be encouraged to change. Radicals need to be taught caution. All change is not necessarily good; people are good.

Table 2.2. *Comparison of the types*

Traditions

The Free Evangelical Lutheran Church of Finland – Vaapakirkko – has many traditions. As a nineteenth century breakaway from the main Lutheran Church it has a reputation for fundamentalism, evangelism, mission and committed involvement of its members. As with other churches in Finland and Scandinavia in general it has benefited over the last 100 years from a series of revivals, great movements of the Spirit of God which have renewed the Church and given rise to periods of rapid but unsustained growth.[10] See Figure 2.4.

Faced with a continuing decline in numbers in recent years and a general aging of the Church membership, the Leadership Council of Vaapakirkko sought to review and renew its vision. I was asked to work with the Council Chairman and the full time staff of the Church's headquarters in order to facilitate the creation of a new vision and structure for the Church. After some eighteen months of preparatory work, discussions, data collection, prayer

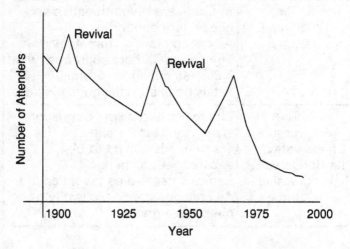

Figure 2.4. *Finnish church attendance*

and consultation, the Council met in retreat to consider the future.

Two days later the group communicated, through translators, their first attempt at summarising their vision: 'By the year 2000, to be known as the church of sound doctrine.' I pointed out that they were already known for that and it hadn't done them much good! After a further reworking the final statement was agreed.

> By the year 2000, Vaapakirkko will be known as the people and the place where love is.

There are traditions older than doctrine! If tradition is important to you then go back to basics. Go back to the foundation of all the law, all the prophets and all the traditions. Love God and love your neighbour as yourself – all else is mere commentary.

Culture, discontent, vision and tradition all need to change if the Church is to fulfil its ministry of change in this generation. The question is 'Will the change be initiated from within the Church in response to a new vision or will it be simply a late reluctant reaction of an increasingly irrelevant institution?' The answer will depend on how we view our church or organisation. But before we move on to look at change and the Church, reflect for a moment on your own traditions.

Reflections on Changing Your Tradition

1. What traditions do we hold that have no scriptural basis?

....

....

2. What traditions do we hold that divide us from other Christians?

   ....

   ....

3. What type of church or organisation are we – Radical, Progressive, Conservative or Traditional? What is our evidence?

   ....

   ....

4. What type of person do you tend to be? Look back at your scores in Table 2.1, page 33
   1. is your Traditionalist score.
   2. is your Conservative score.
   3. is your Conservative Progressive score.
   4. is your Progressive score.
   5. is your Radical score.

   ....

There are some extremes in all of us!

5. How do we treat people whose views of change are different from our own? Give some examples.

   ....

   ....

   ....

   ....

References in Chapter Two

1. St. Matthew 5:43,44
2. The Documents of Vatican II, Geoffrey Chapman, London 1966.

3. ibid.
4. Acts 16:15,19,33,37
5. Russian Orthodox Readings, No. 1, page 4, Pododinskaya, Moscow, 1992.
6. Rostan, Jean, Translated by Saturday Review Press and quoted by C. Everett Koop in *The Right To Live: The Right to Die*, Tyndale House Publishers, Wheaton, Illinois, 1976.
7. HMSO, Charitable Giving in the United Kingdom.
8. Machiavelli, Niccolo, *The Prince*, Penguin Classics, PenguinBooks, 1984, p. 51.
9. Macaulay, Thomas Babington, Horatius, *Oxford Library of English Poetry*, Volume III, page 24, Stanza L, Guild of Publishing, London, 1986.
10. Brierley, Peter, *Statistics of the Finnish Churches*, Marc Europe, 1990.

CHAPTER THREE

CHANGING YOUR FOCUS

O would that God the gift would give us
To see ourselves as others see us[1]

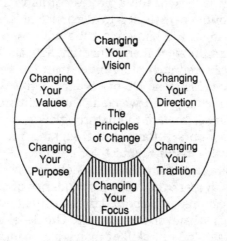

They say the camera never lies. This may be true for your camera but certainly my photos often bear little resemblance to the original! The speed of the subject, camera shake, distance, light and unwanted fingers are all very capable of transforming that prize winning vista into a 'Guess-what-this-is-meant-to-be?' competition! However, now I have one of those idiot-proof cameras which, over the years, has provided me with sufficient recognisable photographic records to invest in an album. That book provides not only a commentary on my changing photographic abilities, it also provides a commentary on change in my life.

Points of Reference

Change has two origins – external change which has its source in the world around us and internal change which comes from our own initiative. We change. The face that looks out from the successive pages of my album is inexorably different. It is older. That face is part of a physical entity which is locked into a process of natural change – from my youth to maturity to decline. For some, these personal changes are harder to cope with than anything the world can throw at them. The fight against the ebbing tide of life can be much more bitter than the struggles to cope with social change. No one wants to give way to the processes which age and weaken. This is understandable, and so cosmetics replace the natural glow of youth, exercise gives temporary tone to the sagging muscles, diet keeps the scales in our favour – for a while.

We all share two common points of reference. Conception and death mark the natural boundaries of the change game. Between these two boundaries we must learn to live with changes whatever their source. Our level of success depends largely on our skill at managing change – a skill which few of us have been taught. Yet it is a skill that we can learn.

Managing Change

'Change and decay in all around I see' wrote the hymn writer of the nineteenth century.[2] For many people that is still true, they associate change with decay. But decay need not be decline. Jesus of Nazareth gave a new understanding to decay when he said 'Unless an ear of wheat falls to the ground and dies, it remains only a single seed. But if it dies it produces many seeds.'[3] With this focus, change is seen as natural, change is inevitable and change can be good. It depends on how well you manage it.

My purpose in putting this text together is that people and organisations might experience change in a much more positive way. My own life has been full of change – many houses, many jobs and many churches as I have travelled around the world. Most of my major changes came by choice and most of them I have looked forward to. I enjoy change. It came as a shock to me to discover that not everyone felt the same way about change! I now know that for half the population change is associated with risk, threat, uncertainty and fear. Of course there have been some changes in my life that I didn't plan – accidents, sickness, conflicts, deaths, financial pressures, business failures and unemployment – all unplanned changes that I would rather not have had to face. These changes too I had to learn to manage and live with. My experience has been that, you can learn to manage change more efficiently both in your own life and in the lives of those around you.

To be competent at managing change is to be competent at living, for life is about change. Look around you. Every day you come in contact with people who have lost the capacity to manage change in their lives. Some of them work with you, some of them worship with you, play golf with you, live near you, or are even members of your own family. For them changes have come too quickly and too often; threatened, disoriented, unable to cope they can go neither forward nor back. They are trapped. Perhaps they are dug in, while around them the real world is changing beyond recognition.

You may be able to manage your change, but you have also a responsibility for your neighbours. They are your partners in pilgrimage. So, not only must you become more skilled in managing your own journey of change, the challenge to individual Christians, the Church and to Christian charities is also to help others regain control of their turbulent lives; to help others manage change.

Why does change disable so many people and not others? Why can some manage and some not? Why are some changes so easy to cope with and others so difficult? Surprisingly enough the answer is simple: like the car on the highway, we can cope with any change so long as we remain in control. It is the sense of loss of control that so many people fear when faced with change. Yesterday we knew how to behave; yesterday we felt capable, confident and comfortable; yesterday we felt valued, but today the situation has changed. Today we feel vulnerable, at risk, out of control. We just need time to think, time to adjust, but time is what we have not got. The changes demand responses now! The decision must be made now! Life must be managed and lived now! But with yesterday's reference points no longer valid, we do not know how to respond or which way to go today.

Perspective

Here is a short important exercise. Please do not move on until you have completed this short task. Think for a moment about your life. Now in the space provided, please draw three circles which represent your life – past, present and future.

Managing change is about managing your life. Life is complex – too complex sometimes, yet most of us manage the complexities reasonably well. To manage all that life throws at us we need access to reference points. Each of us possesses such a concept within our sub-conscious. This reference concept I call your 'life space concept'. Faced moment by moment with life's changes we continually refer to our life space concept in order to make decisions. The three circles exercise is a way in which we can tap into

Draw your three circles here.

our own life space concept. Your own response to the exercise can tell a lot about your view of life and therefore how you approach life and change. But first let me ask you to describe in more detail your life as represented by the three circles.

1. What three different words or short phrases would you use to describe your past life? Write your descriptions alongside or underneath your past circle. Do this now.
2. What three words or phrases would you use to describe your life at the present time? Write the three

descriptions alongside or underneath your present circle. Do this now.
3. For the future circle choose three words or phrases which describe the way you would like your life to be and write these beside your future circle. Do this now.

Life Space Concepts

People carry in their subconscious mind an overview of their life – past, present and future. This is used as an ongoing reference for decision making. Another concept that people use is the idea of 'life span'. Life span has nothing to do with how old you are in terms of your current chronological age. Life span has to do with how old you feel! For example, some people always feel twenty and feel they have their whole life before them, which, by the way is always true – what ever time you have left of your life, you have it all before you! On the other hand there are people who have lived their life under a constant threat of impending death or disaster; for them life has always been closing in, about to shut down any moment. As your life span concept affects your whole attitude to life and change so too, in a more profound way, does your life space concept. The circle exercise gives you some insight into your own perception of your life space.

Let us look at the interpretation of your circles. There are ten basic ways in which you can draw the three circles. These arrangements will give us some insight into the ways that people view life and change. Here are the options.

1. The Static Focus

Here the three circles are all the same size but they do not touch or overlap. It does not matter whether your circles go across the page or up or down. The static view of life is usually drawn by people who are constant and reliable. As things were, so they are and will continue to be, is their belief.

Static circle drawers are predictable and stable. However, they often have one shortcoming, they are not people of vision. It may be difficult for them to imagine a future which is radically different from today. When it comes to change they may have difficulty in seeing the need for it. They value continuity.

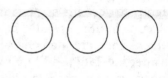

2. The Progressive Focus

Here the three circles are drawn in increasing size from the past through the present into the future with the future being the largest. Once again the circles do not overlap or touch. The progressive circle drawer has a very positive view of life. Things have been good, they are even better now and the future holds great promise.

The progressive person is dynamic, imaginative and creative. Life offers many opportunities and they are anxious to ensure that they embrace as many of these opportunities as possible. However, there may be a problem here. Because there are so many things that could be done, the progressive circle drawer may have difficulties in determining priorities. Of all the things they could do, which one will they do next? This dilemma may cause them to lose focus and attempt to take on too much. When it comes to change, they are likely to overestimate what is possible. Continuity of growth is assumed.

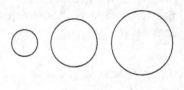

3. Regressive Focus

Here the three circles decrease in size from past to future so that the past circle is the largest and the future circle is the smallest.

The regressive circle drawers tend to be life's pessimists. Their future is all behind them! They are the believers in yesterday. Life used to be very good, but things have deterio-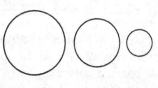
rated recently, and as for tomorrow, well, 'Forward though they canno' see, they guess and fear.'[4] With an outlook like that it is not surprising that these people live in the past. For them the good old days will not come again but that does not stop them trying to revisit them as often as possible. They will be reluctant to think positively about tomorrow and therefore will tend to avoid long or even short term goal setting. When it comes to change, they are likely to underestimate what is possible. This life view is quite independent of age, young people without work and with no prospects or without self-esteem may draw the regressive circles. Continuity is as worrying as it is inevitable.

4. The Transitional Focus

Here the present circle is the smallest of the three. It is not significant if the past is larger or smaller than the future, although a smaller future may indicate a tendency to pessimism.

For the transitional circle drawer, the present is somewhat uncomfortable. Life has been good, and will be again, but just at the moment life has its problems. The problems may be health, work, relational or financial. They are in the valley of shadow, but there is light up ahead and the future looks bright. Transitionalists are usually optimists – things

will get better, but not yet.
Here is the risk for the tran-
sitionalists. They tend to
put things off – only for a
while, of course, until things get better! When it comes to
change they are life's procrastinators – 'Let's wait a while.'
Continuity is on hold at present: normal continuity will be
resumed as soon as possible!

5. The Present Focus

Here, the present circle is the largest. Once again it does not
matter whether the future circle is larger or smaller then
the past circle.

With the focus on the pre-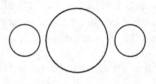
sent, life tends to be very
busy for the present circle
drawer. Yesterday has gone,
tomorrow hasn't arrived yet
so 'Eat drink and be merry
because if tomorrow ever comes we can eat drink and be
merry again!' There is one big problem for the present
circle drawers. For them only today is of significance.
The world is a very uncertain and unpredictable place
therefore for them planning seems to be a waste of time.
The world changes so quickly it is wiser to live now and
plan later. This will tend to make the present circle drawer
somewhat short term in their thinking and more reactive
than proactive. Nevertheless life is fun! Changes are OK as
long as they do not require long-term planning. Continuity
is perceived as irrelevant.

6. The Relative Focus

Here the three circles overlap. You may have overlapped
any of the preceding five forms. If you have then you need
to re-read the previous description coupled with this one.

Relative circle drawers see connections in their lives,

connections between the past and the present and the present and the future. The greater the over- lap the greater the connections. They are where they are because 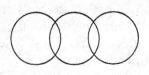 of where they have been and their future is dependant on where they are at present. For them life has its ebbs and flows. There are patterns to life, trends, interconnections and influences. Living in such a complex world calls for caution. Decisions made today will affect their whole future, therefore take care, think it out again. Relative circle drawers tend to suffer from indecision. They need to get things right. Caution is the name of their game. Changes will tend to go slower under the leadership of a relative circle drawer – maybe even too slow. Continuity of activity is paramount.

7. The Integrated Focus

In this form the three circles overlap. The past is over- lapped with the future as well as the present. The size of the circles is of less importance in this form, but where they differ see the earlier descriptions of that particular form.

The integrated circle drawers are somewhat of a rarity – but a nice rarity! They tend to be very sensitive to the feelings of others. They make great team members and good friends. For them life is not so much about 'What' as about 'Who'. The integrated form is an extreme version of the relative form. Not only do they have to consider the past and the future in their deci- sion making, they also like to consider the effects that any change might have on the people around. People come first, the task comes second. This may mean that the integrated circle drawer will avoid taking deci-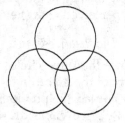

sions or making changes which might have a negative impact on others. Their thoughtfulness helps avoid conflict but their tentativeness may also inhibit change. Continuity of relationship is important.

8. The Expansive Focus

Here the three circles are concentric with the future being on the outside as the largest circle. The circles look like the rings of a tree.

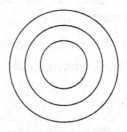

It is an extreme version of the progressive form. The expansive circle drawer is the most dynamic of the ten forms. These people are life's entrepreneurs, very positive in their thinking and often strong in leadership. They are also fast movers – too fast for many people and as a result one weakness can be their insensitivity to the feelings of others. Tasks definitely come before people; in this respect they are the opposite of the integrated form. Although they may make good team leaders, they are not good team members due to their lack of sensitivity. During times of change they are likely to create a number of casualties, forgetting that they need to go at the speed of the slowest. Continuity, like everything else, can get in the way.

9. The Implosive Focus

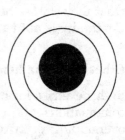

As with the expansive focus the three circles are concentric but the centre circle, the smallest, is the future. This is the extreme form of the regressive focus.

It is often linked to clinical depression and therefore is not a common form. Very rarely, I will come across a person who draws this form and has been thinking of a sporting target when drawing their circles. When it was a target in mind, then the description of the expansive focus applies.

Implosive circle drawers are life's casualties. Life has been good, but that was a long time ago, and now the world is collapsing about their ears. These people do not need more change, they need help to regain control of their lives. It is a very rare form. I have come across it most frequently in the old communist countries of Eastern Europe.

10. The Random Focus

Here the three circles are simply placed at random on the page. Little or no thought has been given to size or position.

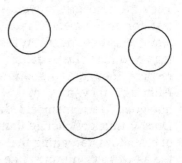

Random circle drawers are life's enthusiasts. They love new things. They will put their energy into any new project – for a while – but they are quick to lose interest. Life has too much to offer to remain committed to one activity or decision for long. Change is their world. If there is no change around, then they create it. However, they often have difficulty in finishing what they start – they prefer to leave the details to others. Continuity is not valued: it may even be despised.

Other Combinations

In this exercise I sometimes come across people who have combinations of forms. For example, only two circles overlapping or two adjacent circles the same size and the remaining one larger or smaller. These represent more complex views of the world, but it is possible to interpret them using combinations of the descriptions already given.

Occasionally you will find people drawing squares, rectangles, ovals, dotted circles etc. I usually just tell them to follow the instructions in future! However, whatever people draw, it is very useful to ask them to explain why they have drawn their forms in the way they have, since this will give greater insight into their attitudes to change.

These circle tests were first developed by Mary Ann Walsh Eells of the University of Baltimore for use in family therapy but their application to churches, missions and organisations is something which I have developed over the last ten years. Later in this chapter we shall see the results of using the circles in relation to the past, present and future of both a church and a mission organisation. Table 3.1 summarises the forms.

Church Perspectives

Gaining perspective is important in managing change. The exercise that you have just completed can be used to help churches, missions and organisations to gain a broad overview of their past, present and future. Instead of asking people to draw three circles which represent their lives, they can be asked to draw three circles which represent their organisation or church. In 1991 I asked a group of some sixty senior church leaders to draw the three circles for the Church in Europe. Table 3.2 shows the results. It was very encouraging to see how many had a positive view of the church's future although 50% drew the transitional form.

The results do not include the response of one arch-

Life space perspective	Form of circles	Stronger features	Weaker features
1. Static		Sense of continuity Stability Reliability	Imagination Vision Risk taking
2. Progressive		Imagination Creativity Vision	Prioritising Realism Pragmatism
3. Regressive		Sense of history Tradition Experience	Positive thinking Goal setting Enthusiasm
4. Transitional		Positive thinking Sense of timing Optimism	Commitment to action Immediacy Sense of urgency
5. Present		Energy levels Pragmatism Action orientation	Planning Forward thinking Continuity
6. Relative		Continuity Purposeful Inter-relatedness	Decision-making Risk-taking Experimenting
7. Integrated		Relationships Team work Interpersonal sensitivity	Taking hard decisions Facing up to conflict
8. Expansive		Dynamism Optimism Enthusiasm	Communication Relationships People
9. Implosive		Sense of history Tradition Pessimism	Positive thinking Goal setting Enthusiasm
10. Random		Enthusiasm Experimenting Impulsive	Planning Continuity Detail

Table 3.1. *Summary of church life space views*

View of the Church	Percentage of Bishops
Static	12
Progressive	8
Regressive	6
Transitional	50
Present	0
Relative	6
Integrated	12
Expansive	4
Implosive	0
Random	2

Table 3.2. *Bishops' views of the Church in Europe*

bishop who drew only two circles because he 'was not going to be there in the future!'

Useful insights into people's attitudes to change can be obtained from the three words or phrases chosen to describe the past, present and future. Examples are given in the following exhibits. Table 3.3 shows the result for a church. See also Chapter Twelve. Table 3.4 shows the results for a mission. Notice in Table 3.3 that the views of the church, as seen by the leadership group, are quite different. Some are positive and some are negative. It is often difficult to accept that the same church can be seen at the same time as 'interesting' and 'dull' and 'together' and 'divided'. Yet if the three circles perspective teaches us anything, it teaches us that we all view the world from very different perspectives. So change must be managed on the basis that people will view the change differently also.

Table 3.4 shows the description used by a mission leadership group. The mission is concerned with young people. Notice the description of the past used by one member

Past	Present	Future
Healthy	Together	Financially
Wealthy	Small	secure
Happy	Divided	Attracting more
Interesting	Under threat	young people
Large	Lacking	Surer of
Institutionalised	commitment	direction
Proud	from many	Friendly
Fuller	Stuck in rut of	Caring
More settled	despair	Loving
Sure of its role	Traditional	Useful
Warm	Caring	More involved in
atmosphere	relationships	national matters
Good music	Poor attendance	Secure in God's
Good worship	Financially	purpose for us
God's presence	insecure	Happy
felt	God's love felt	atmosphere
Dull	Unattended	Freedom to do
Distant	Sad	what we should
Traditional	Awakening	do
Respected	Slow to respond	Welcoming
	On the fence	Outreaching to
	Lost respect	community
		Not being afraid

Table 3.3. *Past, Present and Future descriptions by a church*

'Sanctified, entrepreneurial eccentricity'! This could be translated as 'holy odd-balls doing their own thing' which is not an inaccurate description of many mission workers!

Whatever your organisation, to manage change corporately means first of all to agree together the essence of your history, your present situation and your future.

Having perspective prevents us from becoming inward looking, isolated and driven by the pressure of the

Past	Present	Future
People-centred	Key position	Effective
Schools	Struggling with	evangelism
Camps	size	Understanding
Steadfast	Finding	the times
Staid	opportunities	Dynamic growth
Caring	Profile rising	Continuing
Pioneering	Aware of	profile rise
Bible reading	necessity of	Ability to even
Sanctified	financial	out income
entrepreneurial	survival	Front runners in
eccentricity!	Responsive	evangelism
Love for children	Quality team	Committed to
Bible-focused	Expectant	the power of the
Steady and	Growing in	Bible
steadfast to	bursts	Enabling
principles	Struggling to	Nurturing
Quick, correct	know the way	Extension of
growth	forward	volunteer
Low profile	Growing	models
Sense of family	Varied ministries	Unified vision
Focused goals	Strong finance	Ready for revival
Biblical	Open to change	Mobilising fresh
standards	Caring	volunteer
	Evolving	models
	Frustrated	Urban ministries

Table 3.4. *Past, Present and Future descriptions by a mission*

moment. Perspective also helps us focus on the process of change rather than on the individual steps and events. Managing change is more about the 'how' than the 'what'.

Reflections on Changing Your Focus

1. What three circles would you draw for your church or organisation?

....

....

....

2. What three words or phrases would you use to describe each circle?

....

3. If you are working in a group, share your answers.
4. What themes emerge from sharing your answers?

....

....

....

5. What do these themes suggest for the way ahead for your church or organisation?

....

....

....

References in Chapter Three

1. Burns, Robert, *To a House*.
2. Lyte, HF, *Abide with Me*.
3. St John 12:24.
4. Burns, Robert, *To a Mouse*.
5. Eells, Mary Ann Walsh, *The Management of Time*, Facts on File Publications, p. 25, 1987.

CHAPTER FOUR

CHANGING YOUR PURPOSE

For this reason I was born, and for this I came into the world[1]

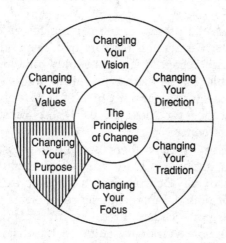

One thing that distinguishes us from the co-created animals is a consciousness of purpose. We, of all God's creation have a sense of future. God has placed eternity in our hearts. 'If only for this life we have hope,' observes Saint Paul, 'We are to be pitied more than all men.'[2] So what are we doing with this unique gift of future consciousness?

Influence

The past, the present and the future are the three great influencers of our behaviour. For some of us the past is the dominant force – traditions guide us, yet they also constrain us. Yesterday's decisions direct us, yet they also bind us. Experiences highlight our memories, yet they also haunt our dreams. Both sleeping and waking, past successes and failures inspire us and inhibit us. We are yesterday's people, products of our past, bound by our histories and yesterday's commitments. Loyalty, faithfulness and commitment to our roots are the most important values for those of us whose past is the dominant influence in our lives.

For others, the present is the driving force. We are the opportunists; we are the reactors and responders to the world around. Yesterday has gone, only today is available and accessible. For us there is no future unless we survive today. 'Give us today our daily bread'[3] is the only prayer of any significance for those of us whose present is the dominant influence.

But in every society there are those whose primary influence is tomorrow. One writer comments: 'The ultimate goals of all societies that have ever existed come from the profound inner experience of some groups of people – religious leaders, prophets, mystic, poet-philosophers, or, in some visionary cultures, the majority of the adult population.'[4] These future-oriented people are the dreamers and prophets of our day. Their daily lives are not lived in the shadow of the past but in the light of tomorrow. Joseph of the many coloured dream coat was such a person. His life was dominated by the future, even on his death bed his eye is firmly fixed on the time when his people will leave Egypt.[5]

The reality is that all three influences – past, present and future – blend together to determine our focus and behaviour. The balance is different in each person, con-gregation and organisation. However it is the future which should be the most important influence when it comes to change. 'Without a vision the people perish'[6] says the prophet, not without tradition nor without a significant role in today's society, but without future consciousness we die.

Alexander Solzhenitsyn has a beautiful prose poem called *The Bonfire and the Ants*. In it he describes the reaction of a colony of ants after their home – located in a rotten log – is thrown on to a camp fire. At first the ants tumble out and find their way to the safety of the forest floor around the blazing logs. But then they circle and seek to return to their doomed habitat. 'There were many who climbed back on to the burning log, ran about on it and perished there.'[7] The ants were wedded to their home. There was no survival outside the colony – even when the colony was doomed and offered only certain death, the ants could not overcome their heritage.

'Where have you come from?' is an important question when dealing with change in the Church. 'Where are you?' is also a critical consideration, but both fade into insignif-icance in the light of the question 'Where are you going?'

Horizon

The answer to the question 'Where are you going?' depends on the time frame that you have in your mind. Let me illustrate. I picked up a couple of hitch-hikers on one of my many trips. They were young Canadians and had just finished travelling around Scotland. I was heading south to London. 'Where are you going?' I asked. Simulta-neously they replied 'Dover!' and 'Round the world!' As we talked together over the next six hours I came to know them quite well. They were both university graduates taking time out to see the world. He was an electrical engineer, she was an agronomist. He was precise and specific in his thinking, she was more imaginative in the ideas she used. He was a short-term thinker and planner whereas her horizons were much longer term – much further out. He saw situations as they were: 'Scotland was cold'. She saw things in context: 'Well, I guess that it was pretty warm considering the latitude and the time of year. That was probably the effects of the Gulf Stream.'

Long-term context and imagination are the key ingredients of vision and to manage change effectively requires longer-term thinking. You need to push out your horizons and consider what may lie ahead. Unfortunately the pressures of daily living often prevent us from taking time to consider seriously what we want from the future. We do not find the time to plan for tomorrow.

We all know the value of planning ahead. We plan our finances; we plan our holidays – often years in advance; we have our career plans and plans for our children's education. Some of us will plan our gardens for maturity – a vision which may take many years to realise and one which we may never see at its best. Business, governments and organisations could not continue without putting a lot of energy into the forward thinking process. Yet, despite these many examples of good, helpful planning practices, few churches today have a clear idea of where they would like to be in the longer term. They take no time to plan for tomorrow's tomorrow.

Language of the Future

There are a number of key words that we need to understand before we can consider the future. The language of the future is simple but the way it has been used in recent years has resulted in a lot of confusion. In *Change Directions* I will use six terms in relation to the future and so we need to define these. The terms are -

1. Purpose = what business you are in
2. Values   = how you run your business
3. Vision   = what you hope for your business
4. Thrusts = what will have to change
5. Mission = how you will realise the changes
6. Goals   = what you will do and when you will do it.

These words are often used loosely and interchangeably. That is unhelpful since each has its own distinct set of characteristics. In this and the next two chapters we shall look at each of the terms in detail and illustrate their importance in the management of change.

Purpose

Your church's purpose is its reason for existence. Why is it there? The answer to this question does not begin with 'Because . . .' Because is a backward-looking word 'Because of the generosity of some long dead benefactor.' or 'Because we were given the land.' The answer to the question 'Why?' should begin with 'In order to . . .' A forward-looking response.

For some folk the idea of applying the term 'purpose' to the Church is very difficult. 'Yes' they say 'It can be applied to companies and organisations of all descriptions – but not to the Church.' Their view is that the Church does not have purpose – only existence. The Church simply is. For them there is no answer to the ultimate question of the Church, life and everything. But Christians and men and women of faith, whatever their belief, should have no real problem with the question of purpose, although they may come up with very different answers!

Much discussion has taken place over the years as to the purpose of the Church. One way to identify the purpose of the Church is to ask what its leadership is being trained for. One researcher looking at theological seminaries, identified five distinct models being used to train church leaders, each model with its own definition of purpose. The five models of the Church were:

1. The Herald of the Gospel to the World
2. The Servant of God's Justice and Mercy in the World
3. The Mystical Communion of the Faithful
4. The Symbol of Christ's Presence
5. The Institutional Community.[8]

You can imagine the quite different teaching content in each seminary! Another way to consider the purpose of the Church is to look at the way it is described in metaphor and simile in the New Testament. There it appears in many forms such as 'salt and light',[9] a building,[10] a body,[11] a flock,[12] a bride,[13] a people,[14] etc. Clearly the model which you hold of your church will significantly influence how you describe its purpose.

Purpose is fundamental to existence. The purpose of an oil company is different from the purpose of a rock band. The purpose of a car manufacturer is different from the purpose of a supermarket. Purposes are long term. They do not change often – or ever in most cases. Having been established for a particular purpose, it is usual for an organisation to remain faithful to that first purpose, although through merger, acquisition, leadership change or crises some dramatic transformations do take place. For example, cinemas have become Bingo halls, churches have become warehouses and now even warehouses are being converted into churches! (However there is a big difference between acknowledging that there is a purpose for the Church in general and accepting that I should commit my energies and resources to the purpose of my own local church.)

Without a clear understanding of your purpose, it is not possible to manage your life or your business or your church effectively, nor indeed to fulfil your ministry as a person or a church.

For a number of years I have been on the Board of Mission Aviation Fellowship, an international Christian mission whose purpose is expressed in the following four-fold statement:

1. To proclaim the love of the Lord Jesus Christ by word, work and deed, and, under God's direction, to demonstrate the concern of Christians for the spiritual, social and physical well-being of all people. In particular, to use our professional expertise in aviation in the extension of God's kingdom.
2. To help the people of the countries in which we fly and serve through the provision of professionally operated and safe aviation transport, logistics, communication services and the development of appropriate infrastructures.
3. To be ready to respond to the needs of relief and development work and crisis situations, working through the local church and other agencies, indigenous or international, as necessary.
4. To identify with the existing Christian Church wherever we serve, recognising our oneness with it and, so far as is possible, to support opportunities for its growth, well-being and expansion.

Yet despite this clear statement, the issues of the mission's purpose kept creating confusion and conflict. You see there is a big difference between an organisation having a purpose statement and having a common sense of purpose. In 1993, as the Chairman of the Board of Mission Aviation Fellowship Europe, I wrote the following to the world-wide membership under the heading: 'Mission Aviation Fellowship Europe is our name, but who are we? What are we?'

1. We are 'mission'. MAF is not just the 'air arm of the Church', or even 'supporters of mission' or 'enablers of the Church' or 'a para-church organisation' – terms often used to describe MAF. We are all of these, but we have been called of God – whatever our role – that together we might serve as missionaries, called and sent by God to serve Him as a team. We are mission and our mission is to minister and witness to the love of God through the organisation known as Mission Aviation Fellowship Europe.

2. We are also 'aviation'. Our primary skills and resources lie in supporting, maintaining and flying planes for the extension of God's kingdom. It is true that we are also in the business of communication, transportation and logistics, but our existence owes itself to the flying machine. It is in this area that our distinctive competence lies. Here we must excel, here we must be the leaders and the standard setters.

3. We are also 'fellowship'. It took me some time to come to grips with this concept of fellowship when I first began to work with MAF in the late 1970s. As a specialist in organisations I was intrigued by the idea. It is capable of being understood in at least five different ways. First, that the 'fellowship' refers to the way we relate to one another at the interpersonal level – that is, that MAF is a group of people who have a very special sense of community. Second, that it refers to the way we manage the mission – that is, MAF operates in a unique way and confers membership status – a covenant rather than a contract – on those who serve. Third, that it has to do with the rights of the members of the fellowship – that is, that members of the fellowship have rights and privileges not normally found in an organisation. (For example, they can select their own board members.) Fourth, that it has to do with the way we relate to our customers – a kind of partnership with other missions

and with the whole Church, and finally, fellowship could be related to our supporters – a network of prayer partners sharing a common spiritual purpose.

4. We are also 'Europe'. The Maastricht Treaty may not survive in its present form, but the commitment to community will remain. In MAF we have over 12 nationalities currently serving in the fellowship. To realise the full potential of MAF will require us to successfully face many difficult challenges. It will call for change. It will call for nation to serve nation rather than to seek national or cultural interests. At a time of growing, divisive nationalism, MAF seeks to unite in fellowship. It seeks to serve together.

MAF Europe. Mission? Yes! Aviation? Yes! Fellowship? Yes! Europe? Yes! These four remain, but the greatest of these must be fellowship – fellowship with God, fellowship with each other, fellowship with other missions, fellowship with the whole Church, fellowship with our supporters and fellowship with our customers. It is this focus on the customer that must be at the centre of our concerns. 'I am not come to be served but to serve,' declares the One we seek to follow.

My reason for writing in such a way was to highlight the need to focus on our purpose. Were we primarily mission? Were we primarily aviation? Were we primarily fellowship? And if we were all three, what should the balance be?

The debate over the purpose of the Church is destined to be with us for a long time, for the greater the change in the world around, the greater will be the need to sharpen our understanding of the purpose of the Church and how that purpose should be worked out in this generation.

Corporate Purpose

Purpose answers the question 'What business are we in?' The answer should be produced as a statement for communication to all who work with or for an organisation. Thus a Corporate Purpose Statement describes the business that you are in. Producing this statement is not as easy as it sounds. For example, what is the purpose of a school, college or university? What is the purpose of a church? What is the purpose of a hospital, the armed forces, social work departments, etc? Clearly there is a lot of room for debate – and disagreement.

Often the purpose depends on the horizon chosen. Thus the purpose of a business may be to survive, pay off the bank loan, make profits for the shareholders, provide long-term employment, contribute to society at large and to serve its customers. Most companies choose to describe their purpose in terms of the shareholders' requirements. However there has been a move in recent years to widen this focus to include all the 'stakeholders', ie those who have a stake in the business, including employees, the trade unions, the community, etc.[15] Here is an example of a Corporate Purpose Statement which embraces the shareholders and some wider stakeholders.

> Our purpose is to provide a superior return to our shareholders by the provision of quality products and services to our customers and through team effort among our people.

Creating a Purpose Statement

The leadership team of the Scripture Union in Scotland met in the mid-1990s to prepare a new strategy for the movement. What was the business that they were in? The group prepared the list as shown below:

Working with young people and their families;

Encouraging personal faith in Christ;

Promoting the Bible and prayer;

Building positive attitude to the Church;

Discipleship, growth, training and equipping.

The group worked on the list and from this emerged the Purpose Statement:

> To enable children, young people and their families to come to faith in Jesus Christ and to help people of all ages, through daily Bible reading and prayer, to grow and serve God as disciples through the Church.

Purpose Statements are not easy to produce. It takes most groups about 3 to 6 hours over a period of two days to clarify and reduce the ideas to a statement similar to that shown above. For Scripture Union, the process of refinement continued over a period of a year as the statement was communicated to and worked on by its Council, staff and volunteer leaders.

Producing the Purpose Statement may take a lot of time. However, it is a vital and basic building block for change management. Some of the common errors that groups make when trying to describe their purpose are to produce:

1. A statement of goals only, for example 'To be the best';
2. A statement of relationship imperatives only, for example 'To work together in harmony and fellowship';
3. A wish list from the leadership, for example 'To eliminate all inefficiencies and get everything right first time';
4. Too general, for example 'To glorify God';
5. Too specific, for example 'To increase giving by 5.3%'.

Purpose is the 'name of our game' – the business we are in. It is related to the other main change terms as shown in Figure 4.1.

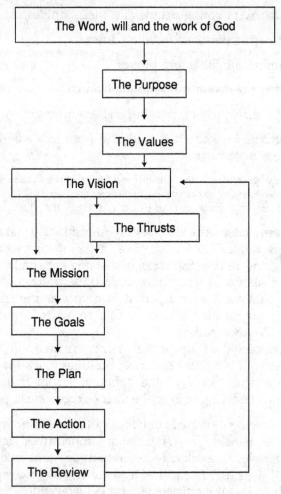

Figure 4.1. *Putting purpose in context*

Each church or organisation must manage change in ways that are consistent with the Word, will and work of God as interpreted by their own theological frame of reference. It is from this frame that their understanding of their purpose will flow.

Each element of the framework will be expanded in subsequent chapters.

Reflections on Changing Your Purpose

1. What is the purpose of your organisation or church?

....

....

....

....

2. How many people in your organisation/church would know your view?

....

3. How many people would agree with your view?

....

4. What process could you use to establish an agreed Purpose Statement for your organisation/church?

....

....

5. What does Romans 9:17 suggest to you about purpose?

....

....

6. What does Jesus describe as his purpose in John 12:27?

....

....

References in Chapter Four

1. St. John 18:37.
2. St. Paul, 1 Corinthians 15:19.
3. St. Matthew 6:11.
4. Harman, Willis, Knowledge for The Future, in *Harvard Business Review*, 1984.
5. Genesis 50:25.
6. Proverbs 29:18.
7. Solzhenitsyn, Alexander, *Prose Poems*, p. 238, The Bodley Head Ltd, 1974.
8. Bunting, Ian, *Places to Train*, Marc Europe, 1989.
9. St. Matthew 5:13, 14.
10. St. Paul, 1 Corinthians 3:9.
11. St. Paul, Ephesians 1:22, 23.
12. St. Peter, 1 Peter 5:2.
13. Revelation 19:7.
14. St. Paul, 1 Corinthians 16:1.
15. Drummond, John, *Good Business*.

CHAPTER FIVE

CHANGING YOUR VALUES

By an accident of history, we in the West have evolved a culture that separates man's spiritual life from his institutional life.[1]

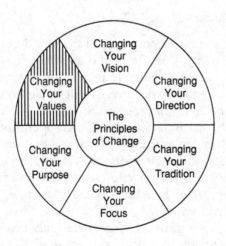

Once the purpose or the 'business' of the church or organisation has been clarified, we can go on to decide how we want the business to be run. We run our lives according to our principles. These principles which guide our behaviour are our values. Values are what we believe in. It is only in recent years that the topic of values has appeared as a significant element of course content in our leading management schools. Unfortunately, leadership values as a topic is still lacking from most theological seminaries and how many of us have had more than one day's exposure to lectures on business or organisation values? How many of us could even articulate clearly the values and beliefs that underpin the practices of our churches, missions or organisations? My experience with many business leaders, Christian and non-Christian, is that less than one in a hundred would be able to list their corporate values from memory!

Values Vacuum

This values vacuum also occurs in the world of the Church and Christian mission. True, the application of Christian values to personal behaviour is often preached and debated, but rarely do Presbyteries, Deacons' Courts, Parish Councils, Committees or Boards consider the application of Christian values to their own operations and few have spelt out in writing the values that they seek to pursue as they do their business. Yet such statements are proving very helpful for churches and mission organisations as they seek to adapt to the challenge of the late twentieth century.

However, we must differentiate between having a 'Values Statement' and having a 'Sense of Values'. Unfortunately, there are many businesses, missions and churches which have Values Statements which bear very little resemblance to their behaviour. Missions which claim to show the love of God to the world can tear themselves apart in internal conflict, while churches which claim to offer acceptance to all are highly selective when it comes to membership. There can be a very big gap between what you say and what you actually do. It is the latter which shows your real values.

Japanese Business Values

During the 1980s Western business managers put a lot of time and money into the study of Japanese business philosophy and found there some widely held and practised values. These Japanese beliefs and values seemed to underpin the Japanese miracle of unparalleled excellence in high quality, high value goods. This of course was not always the case. In the 1950s and 1960s, Japanese goods would have been described as cheap, unreliable copies of the best in the West. But within 25 years Japan had taken the lead in many areas of technology. This success is widely attributed to their ability to apply their values in the work place. Three of these values have relevance not only for Western business, but for the Church.

The Japanese have a strong belief in their destiny as a world power.[2] They believe that the potential of Japan and the Japanese is unlimited. Compare this with the thirty years of decline in Britain as a world power. It is also in stark contrast to the declining place of the Church in Western Europe and the loss of vision in our congregations and in so many of our religious leaders. Christians need to live in the light of their destiny. The Church needs to rediscover its standing in Christ.[3] It needs to teach the value of the soul.[4] It needs to help its members rediscover their personal and corporate destiny in Christ.[5]

The fundamental Confucian value of filial piety is the second of these great Japanese beliefs.[6] It shows itself in loyalty to the family, to colleagues and a life-long commitment to the organisation and its employees. Compare this with the tragic experience of so many congregation members in Britain and Europe who have experienced decline in commitment in a society in which corporate and congregational loyalty has little or no meaning for the majority of the church attenders. It is sad, but of little wonder that when disagreements arise in congregations a switch of churches is so often chosen as the way ahead.[7]

The third great underpinning value of the Japanese is the Confucian concept of 'continuous improvement'[8] – yes the Japanese have been at it for 2500 years! Compare this with our own preoccupation with tradition and maintenance and with short-term survival rather than long-term growth. And yet the Christian faith is developmental in nature. We are being renewed daily.[9] We are being transformed.[10] We anticipate change.[11] Continuous change is our agenda too or should be!

Western Values

Destiny, loyalty and change; these are some of the values which have made and are continuing to make Japan great. Now I know that from our Western Christian perspective, there are some very negative and worrying values associated with the Japanese. Japan is the greatest non-Christian economic power in the world and its non-Christian values permeate its culture. Male/female differentiation is fundamental to Shintoism the main religion of Japan. The Institute for Research on Intercultural Cooperation describes Japan as the society with the highest 'masculinity index' – a measure of the degree of social role division between male and female.[12]

Quality of life in Japan is often poor due to the overcrowding around the major cities, with living space at a premium. Restricted trade practices are rife and threatened US/Japanese trade relations in the mid 1990s.[13] Youth alienation is high and suicide rates among the young are the highest in the developed world. Their value system places expediency before conscience in decision making. Japan's legal process has no jury system and its record of human rights has not been good, but its giving to international relief work is now the highest per capita in the world.[14] Japan has a lot to learn, but learning is one area in which the Japanese have already proved their excellence. Now, I am not suggesting that we adopt Japanese values. I am asking that we rediscover our own values, live by them, teach them and through them provide a new input to our churches and organisations from which excellence might grow. This is the message of St. Paul in 1 Corinthians chapter 13; the more excellent way is not based on gifts, but on values. It is our values and beliefs which determine our actions.

Four Values Worth Building On

If the values of national pride, loyalty, commitment to others and continuous improvement are reflected in Japanese practices, what values do you see reflected in the practices of church and mission leadership and membership in the West?

Do our congregational values provide us with an appropriate foundation upon which to build excellence? Are our values worth building on or do they need to be restructured? Do we even know what our values are? Of course, as Christians we believe in the importance of personal, corporate and societal growth but have we developed a set of practices which promote these values? The answer, unfortunately for most churches must be 'No'.

How can we develop widespread commitment to the growth of individuals in the Church today? How can we develop loyalty to the Church, loyalty to our fellow members and commitment to cooperation with others, rather than the commitment to self-interest, destructive interpersonal competition and a general disregard for the rights of other members of the Body of Christ? One way is to teach the missing values which would promote these behaviours.

I believe that there are four values which the Church must more actively teach and practice today if we are to recover our ministry of change.

First, the value of personal worth and self-esteem based on the uniqueness, significance and importance of the individual. The Church exists for the people, not the people for the Church. Whatever the purpose of the Church it is there for its members as part of the Body of Christ.[16]

Second, the value of loving our neighbours, of esteeming them and promoting their growth and well-being rather than pursuing our own interests at the expense of those around us. The Church as a community exists to bear one another's burdens and to provide an environment in which people can grow and be built up in love.[17]

Third, the value of community and of the consequent responsibility of the Church to take the need for social and human change into account when considering the future. To whom is your Church or organisation accountable for its changes on a practical, day-to-day level? How is that accountability exercised? Too often the concept of accountability is a loosely expressed spiritual platitude which denies our accountability to one another as our brother's keeper.[18]

Fourth, the value of personal and corporate vision and the importance of our personal and corporate responsibility for tomorrow as well as today. Some traditions are committed to passing on their faith in a very structured way to the next generation. The Passover[19] and Communion[20] are examples of forward looking traditions. But few would deny that this forward looking value has largely disappeared from personal practice in our enterprising, self-seeking, Western culture and even, to a large extent, from the Church. Who is demonstrating to us the importance of personal and corporate vision and who is championing the need to provide not only for ourselves in this generation but the need to lay a surer foundation for tomorrow's Church, tomorrow's communities and tomorrow's Christians? Who is passing on the Church's tradition of change?

Propagators

Fewer than 10% of the UK population attend church regularly.[21] The position is much worse on mainland Europe. With this state of affairs we cannot expect the next generation to adopt the values that Christianity offers and teaches. Even those who profess Christianity seem to be largely locked into a 'Sunday only' trading concept, their faith being largely irrelevant to their business and home life. Although 80% of the population still claim to be 'Christian'[22], what this means in practice is regular Sunday teaching in the faith for one in three in Northern Ireland[23], one in five in Scotland[24] one in ten in England,[25] one in twenty in France,[26] and less than one in forty in Scandinavia.[27]

In schools, Religious Education is no longer a significant medium for passing on the values and beliefs of society. We cannot expect schools in the future to be the providers of Christian values. The new curriculum places emphasis on literacy and numeracy but not on the teaching of values. In 1994 the Church of Scotland General Assembly was shocked to find that its own expert committee on Religious Education in Schools had actually agreed to a syllabus which allowed religion to be taught 'without mention-ing God.'[28]

The third propagator that we perhaps could hope would pass on our values is the family, but that once secure base of Western society seems to have lost its capacity to hand on the values of life-long commitment and loyalty. Self-interest, intolerance and self-gratification rules OK!

Yet we know what the values should be. Publicly we affirm them. The problem is that too often we do no more than affirm our values. We fail to practice, promote, teach and develop them.

Four Action Points

Practically, what can we do? Let me propose a number of actions for you and your church. Every one of these proposals is based on current and developing practice in the UK, the practice of a few churches and missions who are pioneering the potential of following explicit corporate and personal values as a means of promoting change within their organisations. The actions fall into four main categories.

First, establish a set of corporate values and seek to operate consistently within these corporate values. Second, seek to create a leadership style which serves. Third, translate the values into learning goals for every ministry and every member. Fourth, establish new measurement criteria which can be used to assess corporate and personal performance in relation to values, style and learn-ing. Let us look briefly at each.

Corporate values

First, establishing a set of corporate values. More and more churches and missions are becoming concerned that they are exposed to unacceptable risks because of the potential for ill-advised behaviour on the part of their leadership and membership. The American TV evangelist scandal which rocked the evangelical community in the early 1990s illustrated just how far adrift Christian enterprise can go when it operates apart from its values base.

In attempts to provide a set of guidelines, organisations have produced statements of 'Operating Philosophy'. These cover the purpose of the organisation, and the values it wishes to hold in pursuit of that purpose.[29] Such statements are not a set of rules or laws within which people are constrained, but rather they are enabling and empowering guidelines which emphasise the spirit rather than the letter of the statement. A number of businesses are producing corporate philosophy statements as part of their initiatives to improve the quality of their service. [30]

A serving leadership

Second, create a leadership which serves. This is a fundamental value in Christianity. Leadership is there for others. To manage is a privilege not a perk. Your commitment to your people must be seen not only in the challenges that you set in your vision, but in the example of your behaviour. The prime customer for the leadership is the membership. In this context, churches and missions have been revising their understanding of leadership and restructuring their activities to provide greater partnership through teamwork and involvement. In the conclusion of his book 'The R Factor', Michael Schluter of the Jubilee Trust in Cambridge calls for new relationships to be established. He calls for 'a second renaissance . . . to rediscover, re-evaluate and rejuvenate relationship.'[31] In this respect leadership must lead.

Ideas into actions

Third, translate your values into behaviours. This is being done through the provision of personal goals designed to develop personal gifts and skills so that all may function effectively as part of the body, from the few in leadership to the many in membership. To assist in this process, everyone in the organisation or mission has their development needs assessed annually and a personal training plan is drawn up with learning goals. These goals are designed to contribute to the individual's personal growth and sense of self-worth so that the search for continuous improvement embraces the being as well as the doing.

Ongoing assessment

Fourth, create new ways of judging corporate and personal performance. How do you assess the performance of your church or mission – by gift income, by progress against objectives, by membership roll levels or by all of these and other objective measures? The time has come for churches to develop new measures of performance, measures which will let us know how well we are performing against the values of the church.

The challenge to Church and mission leaders is to rediscover the power of values to underpin, guide and promote change. Christians have a rich and varied heritage of spiritual values. To lead our churches and missions without reference to these fundamental concepts is like running a nuclear power station without the fuel rods – it's safer, but it never works very well!

Many values from the business world are similar to those from the world of faith. Basically values are what we believe in. The Scripture Union in Scotland produced an initial list of 20 values as shown.

Christian Organisation Values

We believe in . . .

1. Caring for our staff and one another
2. Developing gifts and releasing talent
3. Our responsibility for the world-wide family of SU
4. Changing willingly under God's guidance
5. Reflecting the joy of the Lord in our work
6. Excellence in all we do
7. Equality and value of the individual
8. Having a cooperative spirit toward those whose values are compatible with SU
9. Prayerful dependence on God in every area of corporate life and ministry
10. Being good and efficient managers
11. Fairness in decision making
12. Consistency in decision making
13. Partnership between staff, volunteers and churches in decision making
14. Appropriate, relational and practical ministries
15. Opening ourselves daily and together to God
16. The power of the scriptures to orchestrate our thinking and decision making
17. Integrity in all we do
18. Being supportive, forgiving and encouraging
19. A family dimension to our organisation
20. Being within the letter and the spirit of the law

These twenty statements were grouped together under four headings. What We Do, Spiritual Nature, Internal Relationships and External Relationships. The emerging Values Statement was then produced.

Scripture Union In Scotland
Values Statement

DEPENDENCE

As a movement we affirm our prayerful dependence on the living God and our commitment to change as we open ourselves daily to Him through the Bible.

WORTH

We affirm the worth of all individuals.

INTEGRITY

We are committed to the pursuit of excellence with integrity in every area of work:

- as a Mission to be relevant, practical and relational;
- as a Company to be law-abiding, professional and efficient;
- as an Employer to be fair, responsible and considerate.

PARTNERSHIP

We value:

- the partnership between paid staff and volunteers in decision making and ministry.
- a working environment which fosters care and support, encouragement and forgiveness and promotes the development of gifts and the realising of potential.
- the relationship with the SU family world-wide.
- the partnership with churches and Christian organisations leading to mutual trust and cooperation.

We can also derive a set of values for a local church and for a business.

A Church Values Statement

As the Body of Christ we value:

1. Our Relationship with God and our personal and collective pilgrimages as we pursue God's calling in our lives.
2. Our Relationships with each other and the active demonstration of our love and care for one another as brothers and sisters in Christ.
3. Our Relationships with and involvement in other churches and denominations which foster Christian cooperation and joint action.
4. Our Place in the local community and the opportunities to serve our neighbours whoever they may be and whatever their need.
5. Our Fellowship with the Church world-wide and our responsibility to share and learn together for the glory of God and the extension of His Kingdom.

A Business Values Statement

We believe:

1. In making the customers king by meeting their physical and emotional needs.
2. In continually developing through innovation and improvement.
3. In team work and cooperation as we seek to achieve our common goals.
4. In empowering one another to give greater service satisfaction.
5. In training and career development for all.
6. Thrift pays and brings great advantages by many small individual steps to control costs and gain sales.

Values in a Christian Context

For those organisations wishing to explore their values and produce a values statement, there are certain guidelines. The book Good Business is a useful reference.[32]

Producing a values statement – some guidelines

1. Values should clearly define the nature of your fundamental relationships.
2. Values should be universal and general rules of conduct – that is, rules that are binding on all members and ministries.
3. Values should focus on right behaviour rather than on avoiding wrongdoing.
4. An effective Values Statement will define 'right behaviour' as 'the behaviour which optimizes all members' benefits and thus makes relationships harmonious, constructive, and mutually beneficial.'
5. Keep the number of core values to around 7.
6. Make them memorable.
7. Communicate them.

Values, beliefs and ethics are not often on the church or mission board meeting agenda, but if change is to be the name of the game this reticence must alter. Below are some of the values common in business value statements.

1. A belief in being 'the best';
2. A belief in the importance of people as individuals;
3. A belief in superior quality and service;
4. A belief in the importance of open communication;
5. A belief in the importance of economic growth and profits.

Summary

Values are those guiding principles which direct our decision making and behaviour. Every church and organisation and individual has a set of values. They are often covert and vary dramatically from the stated values. We say one thing but do another. I recommend that all organisations examine their values, commit them to paper and communicate them to all members.

Organisations should assess their performance against their values annually.

Reflections on Changing Your Values

1. What values does your organisation or church use to guide its behaviour?

   ....

   ....

   ....

   ....

2. How many people in your organisation/church would know your view?

   ....

3. How many people would agree with your view?

   ....

4. What process could you use to establish an agreed set of values for your organisation/church?

   ....

   ....

   ....

References in Chapter Five

1. Athos and Pascale, *The Art of Japanese Management*, Simon and Schuster, New York, 1981, p. 192.

2. Horsley and Buckley, *Nippon New Superpower*, BBC Books, 1990, p. 258.
3. St. Paul, Ephesians 1:4.
4. St. Paul, Romans 5:8.
5. St. Paul, Colossians 1:27.
6. Rauch, Jonathan, *The Out Nation*, Harvard Business School Press, Boston, 1992, para 71, p. 68.
7. Gibbs, Eddie, *How to Reach Nominal Christians*, MARC Europe, 1989.
8. Horsley and Buckley, *Nippon New Superpower*, BBC Books, 1990, p. 213.
9. St. Paul, 2 Corinthians 4:16.
10. St. Paul, 2 Corinthians 3:18.
11. St. Paul, 1 Corinthians 15:51.
12. Hofstede, Geert, The Cultural Perspective in *People and Organisations Interacting*, John Wiley and Sons, 1985, p. 227.
13. Horsley and Buckley, *Nippon New Superpower*, BBC Books, 1990, p. 255.
14. Horsley and Buckley, *Nippon New Superpower*, BBC Books, 1990.
15. St. Paul, 1 Corinthians Ch. 15.
16. St. Paul, Romans 12:5.
17. St. Paul, Ephesians 4:16.
18. Genesis 4:9.
19. Exodus 12:14.
20. St. Luke 22:19.
21. Brierley, Peter, *Prospects for the Nineties*, MARC Europe, 1991, p. 20.
22. Gibbs, Eddie, *How to Reach Nominal Christians*, MARC Europe, 1989.
23. Brierley, Peter, *Prospects for the Nineties*, MARC Europe, 1991.
24. Brierley, Peter, *Prospects for the Nineties*, MARC Europe, 1991.

25. Brierley, Peter, *Prospects for the Nineties*, MARC Europe, 1991.
26. Brierley, Peter, *French Church Review*, MARC Europe, 1990.
27. Brierley, Peter, *Finnish Church Review*, MARC Europe, 1990.
28. General Assembly of the Church of Scotland, 1994.
29. Royal Dutch Shell Group of Companies, *Business Principles and Practices*, 1986.
30. Royal Bank of Scotland, *Customer Charter*, 1993.
31. Schluter and Lee, *The R Factor*, Hodder and Stoughton, London, 1993, p. 271.
32. Drummond, John, *Good Business.*

CHAPTER SIX

CHANGING YOUR VISION

If you have no vision, what will you tell your children around the fire in the long dark winter night? (American Indian Proverb)

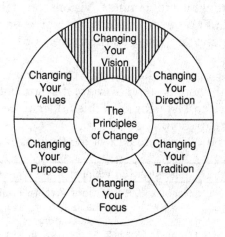

There is a danger in a fast moving society that change gives the impression of progress and that movement implies vision. However, any dead fish can go with the flow. Change is indeed needed but it is not sufficient in itself. We also need vision otherwise we are at the mercy of uncontrolled forces in society at large. 'Without a vision', the wise man warns, 'the people perish.'[1]

We can understand the importance of vision for God's

people simply by reference to Scripture. God is the giver of vision.[2] His people are the people of vision.[3]

Future-orientation

Visions are future-oriented – they indicate what is to come. Sometimes the vision is followed quickly by its own fulfilment, as in Acts when St. Peter is given the vision of the unclean animals. Within minutes the meaning of the vision is made clear.[4] On other occasions the fulfilment of the vision takes years as in the visions to Pharaoh when seven fat cattle and seven lean cattle predicted a 14-year cycle of weather: drought and famine.[5] Visions can take generations to fulfil[6] or even millennia.[7] However, most frequently visions are used to promote hope, inspiration and action.

The terms 'dreams' and 'visions' both occur in Scripture and although there is some overlap, they are both used by God to speak to His people[8.] Table 6.1. may be used as a useful differentiation.

Dreams and visions are part of the language of the Holy

Dreams	References	Visions	References
1. Often need interpreting.	Genesis 40:8	1. More likely to be self explanatory.	Habakkuk 2:2
2. Often for personal consumption.	Genesis 28:12	2. More likely to be for society.	Ezekiel 2:3
3. More frequent than vision.	Genesis 37:9	3. Less common.	1 Samuel 3:1
4. Given for reflection.	Daniel 9:23	4. Given for action.	Acts 11:12
5. Products of the mind during sleep.	1 Kings 3:15	5. Products of the Spirit when awake.	Revelation 1:10

Table 6.1. *Comparison of dreams and visions*

Spirit, and as such are subject to the Word, will and work of God. However there are some features which will help us recognise visions from non-visions. I use the six letters of the word VISION to characterise the nature of true vision. The characteristics are :

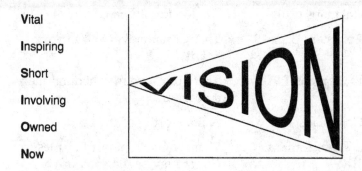

Vital

Inspiring

Short

Involving

Owned

Now

Vital

Vision is at the heart of the purpose of the church or organisation. It is at the 'guts' – the very vitals – of the enterprise. Thus to have a 'vision' for a new car park is a contradiction of terms – unless of course your business is car parks! So the vision should be related to the purpose.

Inspiring

Vision, by definition is inspiring, even awe inspiring. It is not simply another dream. Vision calls for change, not more of the same. It represents a leap in thinking or a discontinuity in development. Consider the letters of St Paul – each one contains what could be described as his vision for his readership. Often these visions are put in the form of prayers since the realisation of vision is dependant on God. The following list shows the inspiring nature of St. Paul's visions for those to whom he wrote.

Romans 15:13	That they might be filled with joy and peace . . . so that they might overflow with hope by the power of the Holy Ghost.
2 Corinthians 13:11	Aim for perfection.
Galatians 6:10	Do good to all people.
Ephesians 3:16–19	That Christ may dwell in your hearts.
Philippians 1:9	That your love may abound more and more.
Colossians 1:10	A life worthy of the Lord.
2 Thessalonians 1:12	That the name of our Lord Jesus Christ may be glorified in you.
2 Timothy 1:13	Hold fast the form of sound teaching.
Titus 1:5	Ordain elders in every city.
Philemon 1:6	Active in sharing your faith.

Short

Visions are to be remembered, recalled, recounted and communicated. They are symbolic of the nature of the future. The land flowing with milk and honey[9] did not actually refer to dairy-produce lakes or apiary surpluses but rather to the nature of the territory. The succinctness of the vision enabled the Israelites to recall and communicate it with ease. If you cannot remember it, it is not a vision. Thus the vision must be written in a memorable fashion. This is usually called the 'Vision Statement'. Here are some examples:

1. *The Arch-diocese of Glasgow.* Through our Renewal Programme, we are moving in Glasgow towards a church

which is: a Community of love, of people who care, responding to the needs of men and women today, guided by God's plan for us.

2. *The Diocese of Arundel and Brighton in Southern England*. By the year 2000 we, the people of Arundel and Brighton, will have learned what it means to be Christ in our world: a community of love, partners in service, a source of hope for all, through God's power working in us.[10]

3. *Scripture Union of Scotland*. Working with the churches, by AD 2000 to be reaching everyone of school age in Scotland with the Good News of Jesus Christ.[11]

4. *Broughty Ferry Baptist Church*. By the year 2000 we aim to be a worshipping, Christ-like, open, caring and supportive fellowship which is committed to faithful proclamation, relevant witness and practical living of the gospel in the community.[12]

5. *Gospel Literature Outreach*. To have 100 evangelism teams in Europe by the year 2000.[13]

6. *Stakis Hotels plc*. By the year 2000, Stakis will be recognised as the best UK hospitality provider.[14]

Because the vision is for the whole community it means that the whole community must be able to understand it. Old and young, mature and immature must be able to identify with the core of the vision. In one cathedral the vision was presented to the congregation in symbolic forms using collages which the children had prepared in response to their understanding of the vision.

It is not uncommon for Vision statements to be expanded for communication purposes. The following expansion from Broughty Ferry Baptist Church, example 4 above, illustrates this:

Worshipping. Putting God and his will first, at the centre of our life, as a church and personally; expressing, exploring and extending our faith through vital and joy-filled celebration for the whole church family in grateful praise, prayer, listening and openness to God.

Christ-like. Living out of deep trustfulness and loving responsiveness to God; acknowledging God as source of all good and being available for his loving Spirit to live his life through us; displaying the fruit of the Spirit – love, joy, peace, patience, kindness, goodness, faithfulness, gentleness and self-control.

Open. Welcoming and friendly, generous in spirit, tolerant, accepting and cooperative; ready for positive change and innovation; given to developing and venturing into new areas of activity and service; available for the new things God wants to do among us.

Caring. Sensitively and discreetly attentive to other people's real needs; bearing one another's burdens, sharing one another's joys; generous with encouragement, patience, forgiveness, comfort, practical help, a listening ear and an understanding heart.

Supportive. Being present to, being with and being for each other and all who are in need; affirming and sustaining other people for their healing and growth; recognising and accepting others as they are, holding them in the love of Christ and seeking their fulfilment.

Committed. Loyal to Christ and his leading; faithful and persevering in following him and seeking to be governed by his Spirit; consistently giving him and his will first place in all decisions and action; making all plans and policies for the sake of his kingdom; dependable and trustworthy in all tasks undertaken.

Fellowship. The shared life of a group of people whose union with Jesus Christ links them deeply to each other in the one Spirit; seeking together what it means to let that Spirit guide and control all their activities; brothers and sisters of the Lord Jesus Christ – therefore, one family in God.

Faithful proclamation. A clear, understandable communication of the good news – true to the biblical message, relevant to the hearers, applied to human need and conveyed effectively to those who need to hear it. The right message conveyed in the right way to the right addresses.

Relevant witness. Pointing people to Jesus as God's answer to their basic need for salvation, wholeness, life to the full; expressing the gospel in deeds that meet people where they are and in words they can find real for themselves; sharing with others the good news and the new life Jesus has brought to us. From experience to experience.

Practical living. Living so that people can see that the gospel makes a difference, issuing in actions and relationships which are relevant to people's needs and which incarnate the love of God for all people of all ages, backgrounds and conditions; alert to discover and quick to do what love requires in response to human need.

Community. Recognising and embracing God's plan for his people as a family and his love for all people; sharing a common life within the church and inviting others to share it too; offering God's love in practical service within the church's neighbourhood; finding and practising ways of being salt, light and leaven within the human family, local, national and international.

Gospel. The good news of life in the Kingdom of God – of forgiveness and reconciliation to God made available through Jesus Christ's atoning death and resurrection; the gift of relationship to God as our Father and life to the full by the Spirit within us; growth into love as we are changed by the Spirit to be like Jesus in our living towards

God and other people; a new living hope of resurrection to eternal life.

Involving

Vision is for the people, for the community. The pursuit of the vision should involve the whole body not simply part of it. Vision must be corporate. No part of the organisation should be excluded from it. It is appropriate for an organisation such as the Boys' Brigade to have a vision which focuses on youth. This is their business. But for a church, youth work is only part of its activities, thus for a church to have its vision focused on one part of its ministry could lead to the neglect of other vital areas.

My own church has recently reformulated its vision. It now reads 'To become an outward looking family church committed to communication and development.' Within this statement the various church organisations are encouraged to describe their own vision and strategies in order that the whole church can pursue the vision together.

Owned

Vision must be accepted by the membership and so they need to be able to identify with the vision. This does not imply that the vision originates with the leader or leadership group. In congregational structures the vision can readily be built from the bottom up. The vision may not come *from* the membership, but eventually it must come *to* the membership. For Moses the problem of ownership was paramount. 'What if they do not believe me or listen to me?'[15] The people would have to believe him in order to identify with the vision and accept it. In many churches and missions the whole membership would be involved in the formulation of the vision thus increasing the ownership of it.

Now

Visions make a difference now. If your church has a vision it will be doing different things. Visions by nature call for change. If there is no change there is no vision. The changes may be small initially, but increasingly the vision will influence the goals, priorities and plans of the organisation.

Thrusts

The above six characteristics can be used to test a Vision Statement. The most common problem is to confuse purpose with vision.

Remember that the purpose is the nature of the business we are in, while the vision describes what we hope to do with our business in the next 5 to 10 years.

Vision calls for change. A vision, by definition precludes simply doing more of the same. In many ways it is easier to get the vision than to realise it because the vision often requires profound, fundamental change which the church, charity or business has had little experience of handling.

To handle the widespread change that is often required by vision it is necessary to group together the many changes into 3 to 5 manageable packages which I call 'thrusts'. Thrusts are areas for change. They are the focus for the initial changes. Like the thruster or booster rockets on a space shuttle launcher, they provide the power to overcome the inertial and gravitational forces seeking to keep the rocket grounded. Organisations are no different from space shuttles: they also suffer from the inertia and the pull of their traditions.

One charity had the vision to double its activities in 10 years. In response to that vision clearly everything would have to change – not only the size of the organisation. Looking at its vision the charity identified 5 thrusts or key change areas. These were:

1. Its visibility with the donor communities;
2. Its relationships with its international partners;
3. Its capacity to use Europe as an integrated resource of funds and support;
4. The quality and structure of its management systems;
5. Its level of skills of management and staff.

These five thrusts enabled the management of the charity to put together change plans for the pursuit of the vision – which, by the way, was fully realised.[16]

Thrusts help you couple your vision to your day-to-day activities and to describe how you intend to pursue your vision.

Mission

There has been a great change in the way the word 'mission' has been used in English in recent years. When I was young a 'mission' was an organisation or even a building. In the inner city streets of the post war Glasgow there were many missions – the Seamen's Mission, the Carters' Mission, the Coal Porters' Mission, etc. Then there were overseas missions – organisations made up of 'missionaries' – people who went away to carry their various messages to other parts of the world. Later, in my childhood reading I became aware of another mission – much more exciting – the secret mission, not a place, an organisation or a people, but a task – something to be done and usually in some distant and dangerous place.

The English word 'mission' comes from the Latin *mittere* – to send, but we have to thank the Americans and the North American Space Administration – NASA – for giving us 'Mission Control' and bringing the word back into general usage as a term associated with risk and achievement.

Mission as a description of a task, implies a temporary

activity. There comes a time when the mission is complete or the form of the mission changes as the world or technology or target changes. Mission is the working out of our purpose and vision in today's world.

In the 1980s businesses began to develop Mission Statements and Vision Statements. Unfortunately the two terms were rarely defined or used consistently.[17] The terms have become interchangeable. But there is one helpful way to create a working distinction.

A *Vision Statement* is a short summary statement of where you want to be in the long term. For example 'To be the best and most successful airline in the world.'[18]

A *Mission Statement* is a short summary of how you intend to realise your vision. For example 'To be the best through dedicated customer care, competitive pricing and excellence in all we do.' This Mission Statement summarises the vision 'to be the best' and the main elements of the company's strategy – customer care, competitive pricing and excellence.

Vision Statements are short; Mission Statements may extend to several sentences or even paragraphs.

Example

The following example illustrates how a Vision Statement and Mission Statement relate to one another. The link is the Thrusts or areas for change.

Vision Statement

'Our vision is to have 100 workers engaged in establishing churches in Europe by the year 2000.'

An examination of the Gospel Literature Outreach organisation in the light of their Vision Statement indicated that a number of major changes would have to be made. These changes were identified as the Thrusts of change for the organisation.

Thrusts

1. Improved recruitment of trainee workers;
2. Increased number of trainees entering GLO;
3. Improved GLO image in the Christian market place;
4. Increased levels of financing;
5. Better international mix/recruitment;
6. Introduction of improved planning structure;
7. Improved use of all gifts especially women's gifts.

Mission Statement

It is only a matter of editing to bring together the Vision and the Thrusts to produce the Mission Statement. 'Over the next five years GLO will realise the vision of 100 workers engaged in establishing churches in Europe by:

1. Reflecting our vision in our image and financial planning. Our financial policy will reflect the support needs of the workers.
2. Changing our recruitment methods to reverse the decline in summer teams and the decline in numbers coming through training into mission teams.
3. Reviewing and revising our representative system to ensure that current and future needs are met.
4. Increasing the level of international recruitment since evangelism is often more effectively done by national workers.
5. Presenting GLO opportunities with training information in order to have more people come forward with their sights set on GLO.
6. Emphasising the need for achievement of goals for church establishment.
7. Improving the presentation of GLO opportunities to students.

8. Creating training and development opportunities beyond the initial training course.
9. Increasing the range of opportunities available to women, particularly women with children.
10. Bringing women increasingly into the decision-making process.
11. Introducing a new structure for planning, reviewing and personal and corporate accountability.

Summary

A clearly articulated Vision and Mission are needed before churches, organisations or individuals can successfully manage change. Vision and Mission are necessary for smooth transition, but they are not sufficient by themselves. Many companies have produced Mission Statements but have seen very little benefit for the considerable effort put into developing them.

Vision and Mission need to be set within the context of the organisation's purpose and values on the one hand and the organisational activities on the other.

Table 6.2 compares the various elements of the forward thinking needed by leaders as they consider the development of their churches and organisations. It shows the difference between the main terms used. Please also refer again to the Framework on page 72.

With Purpose, Values, Vision and Mission now in place we have the 'What?' of change and the 'How?' of change identified, written down and in a form which can be readily communicated. But this does not mean that the changes will be automatically realised. We need to move into action and action requires skill.

In the next five chapters we will look at some of the key skills needed for the successful management of change.

Term	Strategic question	Horizon	Revision period	Quantitative content
Purpose	What business are we in?	Long	Seldom	None
Values	What is important to us in the way we do our business?	Long	Seldom	None
Vision	What do we aim to become in the next 5 to 10 years?	Long	Every 5 years	Some
Thrusts	What areas of our activity will require to change?	Short to Medium	Every 3 years	Some
Mission	How do we intend to realise our Vision?	Medium to Long	Every 3 years	Some
Goals	What will we do and when?	Short	Annually	All

Table 6.2. *Comparison of key terms*

Reflections on Changing Your Vision

1. What is the vision of your organisation or church?

   ....

   ....

   ....

....

....

2. How many people in your organisation/church would know your view?

....

3. How many people would agree with your view?

....

4. What process could you use to establish an agreed vision for your organisation/church?

....

....

....

....

5. What major changes would have to take place before your vision could be fully realised?

....

....

....

....

....

References in Chapter Six

1. Proverbs 29:18.
2. Numbers 12:6.
3. Joel 2:28.
4. Acts 10:17.
5. Genesis 41:26.
6. Genesis 46:3.
7. Daniel 12:13.

8. Numbers 12:6.
9. Exodus 3:8.
10. Diocese of Arundel and Brighton, Vision Statement, 1991.
11. Scripture Union of Scotland, Vision Statement, 1993.
12. Broughty Ferry Baptist Church, Scotland, Vision Statement, 1993.
13. Gospel Literature Outreach, Vision Statement, 1994.
14. Stakis Hotels plc, Vision Statement, 1994.
15. Genesis 3:11.
16. King, Stuart, *Hope has Wings*, Marshall Pickering, 1993, p. 304.
17. Campbell, Devine and Young, *A Sense of Mission*, The Economist Books, 1990, p. 17.
18. British Airways, Mission Statement, 1979.

PART TWO

The Practice of Change

CHAPTER SEVEN

UNDERSTANDING YOUR CHANGES

There is a time for everything, and a season for every activity under heaven.[1]

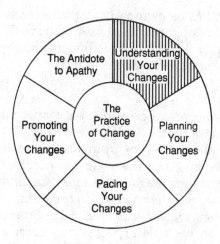

In this second part of *Change Directions* we shall look at some of the key skills needed to manage change effectively. The skills include being able to recognise the different types of change, being able to pace the change at speeds appropriate to the needs of the situation, the capacities to plan, communicate and influence. In this chapter we shall

111

look in depth at the different patterns of change that you may be required to manage.

Patterns of Change

Although most people talk of change in general terms, there are five distinct patterns of change:

1. Cyclical change
2. Linear change
3. Exponential change
4. Discontinuous change
5. Combination change.

Each pattern has its own particular features and presents us with special opportunities and problems. To deal with these effectively it is necessary to understand the pattern of the change. Let us look at each in turn.

1. Cyclical Change

Change is usually non-reversible. We cannot put the clock back. It is only in the fictional world of *The Star Ship Enterprise* that men return from the future to save the whale. In real life, once the event has occurred it is past. But some events occur again and again. Cyclical change is, as its name suggests, change which comes in cycles. These cycles are often regular and predictable occurrences. The seasons are an example of this – they form a repeating pattern – a cyclical change. The effects of cyclical changes are fairly predictable and so we can plan for them. We know, for example that we must expect to spend more of our budget on fuel in the winter, and for most people, the balance of time spent outdoors and indoors varies with the seasons.

There are of course changes which occur in cycles which have shorter or longer frequencies. Day and night is a cycle and just how well we have adapted to the twenty-four-hour cycle is shown by the effects of jet lag when we cross time zones – our body tells us it is one time and our watch tells us it is another – and our body always wins the argument! Our bodies also have energy cycles – times when we are at our best and times when we are at our lowest efficiency. We experience a monthly cycle and some of us are strongly affected both emotionally and physically by the presence or absence of sunshine. The lunar cycle is also reputed to influence people who are abnormally sensitive to the phases of the moon.

Longer-term cycles are less evident, but nevertheless just as significant for us. National economics affect us all and vary in a cyclical, but less predictable fashion. Weather, particularly world temperature and rainfall, varies in cycles which span centuries but are evident in the records of tree rings. All around us and within us, creation ebbs and flows to rhythms which have an unavoidable impact on our lives. For the most part we take these changes in our stride. However there are times of danger. We are at risk when some of these cycles coincide.

Take a simple domestic example. Usually we can cope with our financial outgoings on an annual basis, but when the quarterly cycle of the gas bill, the electricity bill, the telephone and the car tax all coincide on our door mat – then we may have a problem!

The so-called 'mid-life crisis' is a coincidence of cycles. It is a period in both men and women in which the body is going through major physiological changes. But, at the same time the family unit may be experiencing disruption as children leave to make their own way in the world. It is also a time of mental and attitudinal readjustment as the individual attempts to come to terms with the second half of life and the ageing process. Financial readjustments are demanded, social readjustments are required and uncertainty of career and role bring added pressures. Each of

Main features of cyclical change	Ways of managing change
Recurring	Keeping alert to the ebb and flow of the cycles
Predictable	Anticipating the adjustments needed in life style
Common	Recognising that you can learn from others
Universal	Recognising that the effects are different in others
Risk of Coincidences	Pacing the changes and planning for coincidences

Table 7.1. *Features of cyclical change*

these changes we could manage in isolation, but together they may prove impossible to handle with comfort.

There are of course many individual changes which will have great impact on us, for example, marriage, the death of our life partner, redundancy or major surgery. But coincidences of cycles are not rare occurrences, they happen to us all and we need to learn to manage our lives through these periods of turbulence. Table 7.1 shows the main features of cyclical change and some helpful ways to manage it effectively.

2. Linear Change

Many changes come about in a slow and steady manner. Gradually, almost imperceptibly, the transition from one state to the next takes place. Mountains wear down. Linear change is characterised by natural progression and development and often over long time periods, thus linear change gives time for adaptation. Take yourself as an example. You are locked into natural processes of change. You grow, you mature and decline. Day by day as a young teenager you may have longed to be taller. You may have stood against the bedroom door and checked your height each evening and morning but rarely would find evidence of that slow development taking place within. Yet it was there; evidenced in the tight shoes and the sleeves that were too short and the variety of undergarments which no longer fitted.

Organisations also experience linear change. Markets change and values change. Perhaps the changes have been underway for years before they come to our attention. Churches face linear change too – the population changes, and the spiritual condition of society changes from generation to generation. Some churches stay alert to their environment, but many are out of touch and awake to the danger of their irrelevance too late.

Today we face a future which many would say is beyond our capacity to influence because the changes in nature have been so dramatic and are so rapid that there is nothing that governments could do – even if they wanted to – that will alter the course of the ecological death track upon which we have embarked. Yet for most of us the world does not look too different. Pollution, ozone layers, rain forests and species extinction don't touch us. Very little seems to be changing. Yet our evolution is the ecologists' revolution. Linear change is often the easiest pattern to handle, but it can often be the most deadly. The easy pace of the change lulls us into a false sense of security – we can cope. Ask any dinosaur!

There is a lesson for us here. The significance of a change is very different from person to person. One man's relaxed pace brings on another's final coronary. What is rapid change for the traditionalist is little more than business as usual for the radical. Table 7.2 summarises the features of linear change.

Linear change	Ways to manage the change
Slow Development	Develop sensitivity to longer-term trends
Incremental in nature	Keep alert to your environment
Predictable	Develop plans
May mutate into other forms of change	Keep alert for signs of change in pattern
Planning is easy	Learn to cope with the unexpected

Table 7.2. *Main Features of Linear Change*

3. Exponential Change

Exponential change is the most dangerous of the change forms. It usually begins in a small way. It may initially look like linear change, but as Figure 7.1 shows, it then takes on the form of a cyclical change before it shows its real nature – run-away change.

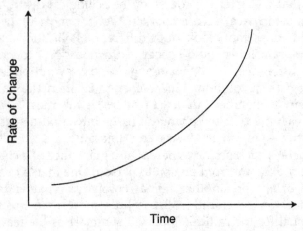

Fig. 7.1. *Exponential Change*

Exponential change	Ways of managing the change
Starts slow	Keep alert for deviations
Confusing signals	Keep records
Transmutes to cyclical form	Take steps to cope with the potential explosion
Changes again to show its real nature	Organise your resources to contain the change
Very rapid final stages	Have contingency plans ready

Table 7.3. *Features of exponential change*

Exponential changes double in size over each successive period of time. Two becomes four; four becomes eight; eight becomes sixteen etc. The spread of disease usually follows this pattern. Rumour follows the exponential curve as does the nuclear explosion – and both are very dangerous!

Managing the exponential change requires a lot of skill, a lot of effort and a lot of luck. Table 7.3 summarises the change.

4. Discontinuous Change

Flying from London to Vienna recently, I experienced a discontinuity. We were flying at 35,000 ft in fairly rough conditions when we hit an air pocket. For most of the passengers, it felt like the end! The pilot later reported that we had dropped 'a little over 5,000 ft' and apologised for any concern that we might have experienced! Discontinuities are bad news for all would-be change managers. To be frank, you cannot manage a discontinuity, you can only manage the after-shock.

Discontinuities come in many forms, but they all come fast! Conversion is a discontinuity, so is winning the pools, getting married, having the first child, changing your job, house or church, being taken over by the competition, and all other changes which require immediate adjustment.

It is the rapid response that makes discontinuity so difficult to handle. Taken by surprise, there is no opportunity to prepare for the changed conditions. We can only react as best we can in the short term and manage the consequences in the longer term.

Catastrophes are discontinuities and by their very nature are nasty surprises! Surprises? Yes, but good news? Definitely not! Death, divorce, bankruptcy, excommunication, redundancy – the nightmare that becomes reality. These are the stuff of catastrophe. Yet catastrophes need not remain tragedies. Talk to many families with a handicapped child and they will tell you of 'that special gift' who came with all the tragedy of a catastrophe and began a transformation process in the family. The Downes syndrome child whose uninhibited love-sharing can change beyond all recognition the typical, reserved family. The spina bifida child whose determination to walk and live a normal life has often inspired families and communities.[2]

Catastrophic discontinuities bring crisis and to deal with crisis needs special skills. Table 7.4 shows the main features of discontinuities.

Perhaps one of the main features of discontinuity is that it is illogical and unreasonable. Charles Handy comments: 'We are entering an Age of Unreason . . . a time when the only prediction that will hold true is that no predictions will hold true; a time therefore for bold imaginings in private life as well as public, for thinking the unlikely and doing the unreasonable.'[3]

5. Integrated or Combination Change

Although I have described these four patterns of change as distinct types, often these become linked to form an integrated sequence of change. A change that begins in a small

Discontinuous change	Ways of managing the change
Unpredictable	Always have contingency plans. What if . . . ?
Sudden	Don't panic
A step change	Accept and work with the new situation
Stressful	Learn to recognise and manage your stress
Loss of control	Depend on God

Table 7.4. *The main features of discontinuities*

incremental manner may suddenly transmute into a new phase and take on the characteristics of exponential change, that in turn may take on the form of a discontinuity or even revert back to linear change.

Table 7.5 gives a comparison of the four main patterns of change which can often combine or interact.

So we see that with integrated change there is no clear distinction between the types. Integrated change embraces linear, cyclical, exponential and discontinuous change. Figure 7.2 on page 121 shows the way in which time, involvement and conflict inter-related for the North American Indian. The same interrelationship holds true for most changes today.

In the history of North America we can see the way that change brought challenge – slowly at first, as only a few intrepid explorers were involved. But as the numbers moving west increased, so the resistance to the change that they represented grew also. There can be no change without conflict. The conflict may be slight. It may be internal as the individual struggles with the options or the fear of the unknown, but the conflict is always there. Or the conflict may be overt and destructive as one great

Type of change	Mode	Effect
Linear Examples – erosion due to weathering; Long-term decline in church attendance.	(graph: Rate vs Time, curve declining)	Predictable rate of change influences how easy it is to manage.
Cyclical Examples – Interest rates in the second half of the 20th century. Church attendance throughout the year.	(graph: Rate vs Time, wave pattern)	Predictable, usually manageable except when cycles coincide.
Exponential Examples – Spread of disease and use of PCs; The growth of the House Church movement.	(graph: Rate vs Time, rising curve)	Often unexpected, early indications may mask potential for rapid growth.
Discontinuous Examples – Oil price rises following war or threat of war in the Middle East; The ordination of women in the Anglican church.	(graph: Rate vs Time, step function)	Unpredictable, traumatic, forces people back on to the defensive.

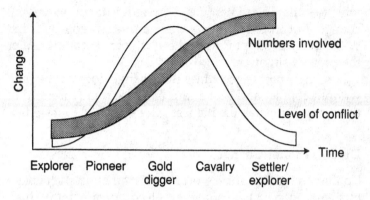

Figure 7.2. *The five phases of integrated change*

nation seeks to dominate another and meets with the opposition of irreconcilable goals.

The Process of Change

This model helps us understand the change process. The explorer teaches us that change will not happen unless someone takes a high risk and is prepared to dream about what might be. It is high risk because the explorer not only dreams but talks about the possibility of experiences as yet beyond the imagination of his contemporary world. Whether the explorer decides that machines can fly, pictures can be transmitted over long distances, women should vote or simply that it is time for change – he or she is a lonely voice. To manage change you must be prepared to put yourself at risk and face the unknown. Remember, the easiest way to recognise the explorers is by the arrows in their backs!

The process of change may be fast or slow. It may take days or years before others begin to listen to your views, but if you persist then eventually the pioneers will join you. Look for pioneers among the discontented. Later we will see that discontent is a prerequisite of successful change, but in terms of the change process you will find your strongest supporters in those who are suffering under the present situation.

It is important to recognise that change does not happen without conflict and cost and it is those in the forefront of the change who pay the highest price – ask any foot soldier.

Organisational Change

Conflict is hurtful, it may even be terminal. In the change business, survival is not guaranteed to any individual, organisation, church or society. Business failures reached record levels in the 1990s and the failures affected organisations of all sizes and in all sectors of the economy.

Studies of organisations show that there is a quite clear cycle of organisation life. This cycle can be described in a

Feature	Stage 1	Stage 2	Stage 3	Stage 4	Stage 5
Name	EXPLORER Stage	PIONEER Stage	GOLD-DIGGER Stage	CAVALRY Stage	SETTLER Stage
Growth rate	High ... Low				?
Primary concern in respect to change	To Discover	To Expand	To Exploit	To Resist	To Renew
Culture	Creative Informal Risk-taking Flexible	Achieving Control Risk-assessing	Optimising Individualistic High risk Uncontrolled	Tradition Loyalty Community Risk elimination	Crisis Vision Leader High risk

Figure 7.3. *The organisation change cycle*

number of ways – according to the organisation's market standing, its size, its strategy, its structure and even how it operates – its culture. Figure 7.3 illustrates some of these features. It shows a five stage description of the cycle of organisation life which closely relates to the main ideas in this chapter.

Which stage is your own organisation or church in at the present time and what features can you identify in your own organisation or church?

Summary

The opening up of the Wild West provides us with one of the classic combinations of the patterns of change. All change seems to conform to this example and has five distinct phases:

1. *The Explorer Phase* in which we become aware of the need for or the possibility of change. During this first phase we may be on our own in our desire for a different world. Few people, if any, will support us or be even interested in our dreams. But if we persist; if we can share our dreams; if we can describe what we have seen beyond the horizon; then someone may listen. Someone may be interested and we can move on together, but if not, then we explorers move on alone. Such is our restless calling.

2. *The Pioneer Phase* sees more and more people joining the cause for change. Often these people are the discontented and the disadvantaged in the present situation but they are the minority – and a small minority. It is easy to explain why they want to change. When Jesus came and preached the Kingdom of God in first century Judea, it was the common people, the outcasts and the poor who heard his message with gladness.[4] In this phase resistance from the majority to the change is still

low, since the pioneer is not seen as a threat to security or the general way of life. However, should the change-makers persist in their efforts, then the self-centred opportunists will begin to espouse the cause.

3. *The Gold-digger Phase* is a high risk period in the change process. By now the benefits of the change will be more evident and people will want to join for what is in it for themselves. In the New Testament, when the early Church was spreading, many people joined for the wrong reasons. In the book of the Acts of the Apostles there is an account of a magician who was amazed at the miracles that the Apostles could do. He joined with the Christians and took the earliest opportunity to try to buy his way into the secrets of the movement.[5] Every change process has been like this, whether it was the Suffragettes, the Trade Unions, the peace movements or the protestor against oppression – of whatever colour – all have attracted people who were interested only in their own aims and who were prepared to use the movement for their own ends. Many change movements have ground to a halt and disintegrated because they failed to recognise and deal with the Gold-diggers. However with alertness to the dangers posed by these self-centred adherents, and with determination, the change process can still progress into the next phase.

4. *The Cavalry Phase* is characterised by conflict. The momentum built up so far can no longer be ignored by those who traditionally have been in control or who have profited from the old ways. Eventually change challenges the status quo. Jesus could stay up in the hill country of Galilee and preach to his heart's content. There he was no threat. But he did not stay there. He took his challenge into the stronghold of the Jewish establishment. He went to Jerusalem.[6] Worse he went into the temple itself and laid down the challenge of change there.[7] Immediately the forces of opposition

Phase of change	Key features	Key skills
Explorer	Unknown territory High personal risk Strong personal vision	Survival Gaining sponsorship Communication of the vision
Pioneer	Critical mass Corporate vision Learning community	Gaining support Learning from experiences Learning together
Gold-digger	Exploitation Conflict Rapid growth	Maintaining control Managing casualties Avoiding rejection
Cavalry	Confrontation Imposition Suppression	Exercising power Enforcing standards Dealing with the resistance movements
Settler	Stability Consistency Conformity	Establishing the new culture Ensuring conformity Finding the new vision

Table 7.6. *Summary of the phases of change*

were rallied. The law and the prophets were trundled out, the Roman authorities were roped in,[8] the traditions of the fathers were lined up all against the one man who was calling for change. Revolutions are made of this stuff. Confrontation is inevitable.

5. *The Settler Phase* lies beyond the conflict. This is the new state where the ordinary people can enter into the benefits of the revolution. Those who were too weak or too fearful to fight for change, can now live and in the peace of the new era, but already the explorers are on the move!

Table 7.6 summarises the phases of change.

Reflections on Understanding Your Changes

1. What changes are current in your life, church and organisation?

....

....

....

....

....

....

....

....

....

....

2. What phases have these changes reached?

....

....

....

....

....

3. What is the next phase that you can anticipate?

....

....

4. How can you minimise the conflict that change may bring?

....

....

....

....

References in Chapter Seven

1. Ecclesiastes 3:1.
2. West, Morris, *The Clowns of God*, Coronet Books, 1982, p. 425.
3. Handy, Charles, *The Age of Unreason*, Business Books Limited, London, 1989, p. 4.
4. St. Matthew 9:11.
5. Acts 8:18,19.
6. St. Matthew 21:45.
7. St. Matthew 21:3.
8. St. Matthew 27:2.

CHAPTER EIGHT

PLANNING YOUR CHANGES

May the Lord make all your plans succeed.[1]

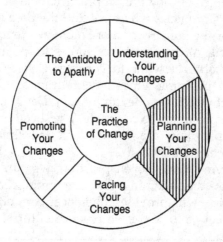

A plan is a bridge between where you are and where you want to be. In my book on time management I identified five features of a good plan.[2] First, it must take account of the long-term vision and the short-term goals. Second, in order to cope with the unpredictable, it must be flexible; a plan does not take the uncertainty out of tomorrow, that is not its purpose. Third, it must be shared with those who will require to implement it. Fourth, it should be the product of team work, not simply the result of one mind thinking. Finally, it should be encouraging and cause its users to persist in the face of difficulty and failure.

Practices

Despite the growing evidence of the importance of planning in all areas of life, including the Church, there is still a reluctance to learn the skills of planning and to apply these skills to the spiritual sphere. Yet the Scriptures clearly indicate that planning is a spiritual activity and give many examples of planning in practice. One of these is in the book of Chronicles where we find the preparation and planning for the construction of Solomon's temple set out as an example of the practice of successful planning.

In this chapter I want to consider seven of the key practices for planning which emerge from a study of this great project which was begun by King David and passed on to his son Solomon to complete. The seven practices for successful planning are revealed in the first book of Chronicles chapters 28 and 29.

By observing these seven practices we can follow an approach to the planning and communication of our change which will provide coherence, commitment and continuity. Let us look at each practice in turn.

The seven practices of planning
Chronicles 28 and 29

1. Planning begins with repentance
2. Planning is an activity of the heart
3. Planning is a spiritual activity
4. Planning is an activity of the mind
5. A plan demands resources
6. A plan demands commitment
7. A plan comes with prayer and celebration

Planning begins with Repentance

A vision and its accompanying plan form the bridge to the future. Not any future, but the one future that calls us with visionary persistence. A plan will not reveal the vision. It is the vision that irresistibly shapes the plan. Unless you have a clear and coherent vision for your life, your church and your organisation, the only plan that should concern you is the plan to obtain the visions!

What gave rise to King David's vision of a permanent place where God should be worshipped? We have to go back to chapter 21 of the first book of Chronicles to find the answer. 'I am the one who has sinned' he says,[3] as he contemplates the horror of the outcome of his ill-considered actions. It was out of his repentance that the vision for the house of the Lord God arose.[4] From Genesis to Revelation, when God gives the vision the people repent and change their ways. Without this repentance or change of mind the vision remains an intellectual concept – good but not good enough.

King David's vision came as a result of a rethink, an 'after thought' if you like. In the New Testament the Greek word is *metanoeo*, literally translated 'after mind' but rendered in English as repentance![5] As a pilgrim people, Christians need vision too. We are the people of the after-mind, the repentance people who daily confess and think again. At the heart of repentance is a desire for change. Those who have no need of repentance have no need of change. To commit to change is to admit the need for a different future.

King David recognised his need for change when he recognised the error of his ways. Those who have no plans for change are not usually short of the skills to produce one, but they are often short of the awareness of the need for the repentance from which the change and the plan flow.

Planning is an Activity of the Heart

Vision is concerned with the future. The emphasis in this sentence is on both concern and the future. Without the concern for today's and tomorrow's generation there can be no Godly vision or plan. Introducing planning because others are doing it, or because the Bishop instructs us to do so is almost sure to fail. Unless you long for the transformation of today's conditions, leave vision and planning well alone.

'May the Lord make all your plans to succeed' is the quote which opens this chapter. It comes from Psalm 20 verse 4, the second stanza. The first stanza is 'May he give you the desires of your heart.'[6] Good plans are infused with the emotions of our hearts. Without the emotional content, the plan is a cold, clinical and lifeless document, ask any Soviet five year planner! King David says 'I had it in my heart to build a dwelling place for God.'[7] Passion is part of planning, not that you believe in the plan, but rather that you believe in the vision that calls for the plan to be produced.

Planning is a Spiritual Activity

It is the Holy Spirit that reveals to us the Word, will and work of God. Discerning the ways of 'the Lord God . . . who is to come'[8] is at the heart of planning. The Spirit speaks to the whole Church and to the whole leadership team as well as to the individual. Have we lost the sensitivity to the voice of God? How can we touch into 'what the Spirit is saying to the Churches'?[9] Unless we listen to what the Spirit says, our plan is no more than guess work.

King David is described as giving to Solomon 'all the plans that the Spirit had put in his mind'.[10] These plans were not broad generalities but contained great detail – sizes, weights, materials, numbers, duties etc. 'All this,' David says 'I have in writing from the hand of the Lord upon me, and he gave me understanding in all the details of the plan.'[11] Without the work of the Spirit the plan would never have been written. Take time to meditate over your emerging plan. Be content with what the Spirit gives, it may be a broad brush revelation as with Moses[12] or it may be a plan in all its detail as with David and Noah.[13]

Planning is an Activity of the Mind

Vision may come through revelation, prayer, listening or simply hard spiritual work, but planning is harder work. Plans do not come with a flash of inspiration as might a vision. The ideas inherent in the vision need to be painstakingly translated into step-by-step actions. It is not everyone who can cope with both the overview and the fine detail. Most people are good at one but not the other. Ideally planning is an activity of minds – plural. If your organisation hasn't got a planning group to help the leadership with its thinking then it is time to establish one. Two or three people would be enough as long as you have both the long-term, conceptual thinkers and the detailed thinkers working together.

A Plan Demands Resources

Time, effort, gifts and support will be required to produce, implement, monitor and adapt the plan. Planning takes time, but it saves time. At least 20% of the period covered by a plan should be given over to producing it. Thus, a ten year plan should take two years to produce, and during this time there is very little to show for the investment. It is clear from 1 Chronicles Chapter 29 that David was a practical planner. He planned with the implementation in mind, 'With all my resources I have provided for the temple of my God,' he says.[14] A plan is a written commitment to the future. There is of course the danger that sitting down and counting the cost will result in a bad bout of panic, but the difference between a spiritual plan and a logical plan is that in the first God will provide, while in the second we cut our plan to fit our panic!

A Plan Demands Commitment

A well-developed and communicated plan creates a positive response. Commitment will flow as the revealed plan rings chords in the hearts and minds of the hearers. Plans are for sharing and the sharing leads to commitment.[15] In his book on visionary leadership, Burt Nanus says:

> People are willing, even eager, to commit voluntarily and completely to something truly worthwhile, something that will make life better for others, or that represents a significant improvement for their community or country,[16]

There will be times when the plan does not go smoothly. There will be times when one step forward means two back. There will be times when it is easier to stay where you are rather than go forward, but with a flexible plan and a compelling vision, commitment will return.

Planning Comes with Prayer and Celebration

The completion of the plan for the church, the parish, the diocese, the country, the mission or the business is a cause for thanksgiving and anticipation. Celebrate your plan. Do not be ashamed of your future. The Cathedral Church of Saint Mary the Virgin in Edinburgh celebrated the completion of a two-year planning process with a dedication service. Here is one of the prayers specially written for the event:

> Almighty God, our heavenly Father, we pray for your Church set amidst the perplexities of a changing order and faced with new tasks: renew us by the power of your Holy Spirit and give us the confidence and vision to bear witness boldly to the coming of your Kingdom, and work faithfully to build it up in this place, through Jesus Christ our Lord. Amen.[17]

This cathedral church used its liturgical traditions to cele-brate with poetry, pageantry and praise its plan for the decade.

The Planning Document

Plans come in all forms and sizes but they flow from the Mission Statement as Figure 4.1. shows. See page 72. A plan requires the organisation and its members to commit themselves to doing new things – more of some and less of others.

In the early 1990s following a three-year period of renewal, the Diocese of Arundel and Brighton in the south of England began a long term development programme. Following a period of consultation by the Bishop, a vision statement was produced and a diocesan-wide strategy for change developed. The vision statement is given below while Figure 8.1 shows the way the strategy for change was initially depicted.

> By the year 2000 we, the people of Arundel and Brighton, will have learned what it means to be Christ in our world: a community of love, partners in service, a source of hope for all, through God's power working in us.

However, a diocese cannot change unless change takes place at the personal and parish level. The larger body can only move forward if all its parts move forward. The keys which open the door to diocesan change are in the parishes, so some tools were developed to help parishes prepare their own plans. One of these tools was a Parish Planning Guide.

The contents of the Parish Planning Guide were designed to help each priest begin to develop or to develop further his parish planning in the light of the Diocesan Vision Statement. Each priest was asked to set up a small Parish Planning Team and to select the one area

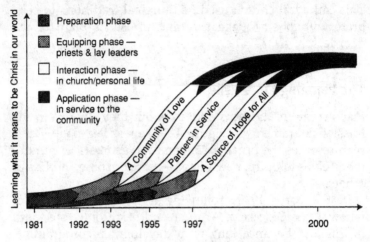

Figure 8.1. *Outline of strategic plan*

of the Diocesan Vision Statement which he would wish to make a priority for his own parish in the next 1 to 3 years. Priests were given the freedom to select another area rather than one of the three included in the Diocesan Vision Statement, if that made more sense. The team was then asked to complete the Parish Planning Guide which is reproduced here.

The completion of these three questions enabled the central Diocesan Agencies to assess the kind of support that would be required of them in the coming three-year period. The remaining questions of the planning guide focused on the work in the parish. Progress toward the vision needs to be measured and so the setting of goals is a necessary step for progress to be measured.

Question 4 requested individuals to take the 8 'more of' or 'less of' statements from question 3 and make them measurable and put a time frame to each as in Table 8.1. These statements with their time frames and measurements can

Parish planning guide

1. My personal priority for my parish is

   _____

   _____

2. Why have you selected this as the priority?

   _____

   _____

3. In order for your chosen area to be developed in the next 3 years please state 2 things which you, the Parish Team, the Communicants and the Diocesan Agencies will need to do more of or less of.

   3.1. Parish Priest:

   i _____

   _____

   ii_____

   _____

   3.2. Parish Team:

   i _____

   _____

   ii_____

   _____

   3.3. The Communicants:

   i _____

   _____

   ii_____

   _____

   3.4. The Diocesan Agencies:

   i _____

   _____

   ii_____

   _____

Statement number	By when	How would you measure progress?
Self 3.1.i		
Self 3.1.ii		
Parish team 3.2.i		
Parish team 3.2.ii		
Communicants 3.3.i		
Communicants 3.3.ii		
Agencies 3.4.i		
Agencies 3.4.ii		

Table 8.1. *Parish Goals*

form the basis of the Parish Plan. They are the 'goals' that the plan should be designed to achieve.

A Parish Plan is simply a way of focusing parish thinking and action on a number of key developments. In Table 8.2 below, Question 5 asked individuals to describe four features of their parish:

a) The present situation
b) The forces helping you move forward
c) The forces hindering your move forward
d) The first steps to take.

In relation to the goal statements in Table 8.1, the four columns in Table 8.2 can be completed for each of the goal statements, two for Self, Team, Communicants and Diocesan Agencies.

Having described the first steps for the eight goal statements, Question 6 dealt with the need to begin to consider what other steps would need to be taken. Considering the

Your goal	Present situation	Forces helping	Forces hindering	First steps
Self: i ii				
Team: i ii				
Communicants: i ii				
Agencies: i ii				

Table 8.2. *Emerging Plan*

first goal statement for the Parish Team, what other steps would need to be taken beyond the first steps already identified if the goal is to be achieved? List the steps in Table 8.3. These steps can then be charted to form the basis of that part of the plan which covers the development and action of the Parish Team. The same should be done for the other seven goals.

Goal	Steps to take	By when
Parish Team i Parish Team ii		

Table 8.3.

Each step can be numbered and marked on a simple chart with a line which shows the beginning of the step and the end of the step as shown in Table 8.4. This was the basis of Question 7.

J	F	M	A	M	J	J	A	S	O	N	D
			2.1	────	──►	2.1					

Table 8.4.

It is important that a Parish Plan assists the Priest and the people and does not become a burden. It is then necessary to schedule the activities, ie. spread them out to give an orderly and manageable plan. Any special resource or support required from the Diocesan Agencies in the parish can then be identified as in Table 8.5. These supporting services or activities should then be communicated to the Bishop's office by a specified date.

Goal	Assistance required
Parish Team i Parish Team ii etc.	

Table 8.5.

Planning guides are very useful for the short to medium term, but for longer-term planning something more sophisticated is needed. A number of church traditions have produced planning guides for the local congregation, among these are the Church of Scotland's 'Missionary Parish', the Anglican Church's 'Parish Audit', the Roman Catholic Church's 'Renew' programme and the Episcopal Church's 'The Purpose of your Church', etc. However, despite all this useful planning material, there is still a great reticence over planning. I believe that the biggest barrier to planning is the fear of failure. People do not like to be seen to be wrong and since a plan calls for goals and timings many people avoid planning or at least keep their plans to themselves!

Scenario Planning

Strategic planning became popular with industry in the post-war period and by the late 1950s most major organisations had set up planning departments. Their capacity to handle change improved when the changes were linear or cyclical in behaviour. Discontinuities, catastrophes or step changes continued to prove very difficult to manage.

The first major, post-war, worldwide discontinuity took place in 1968 with the Arab–Israeli war. The vulnerability of the free world's major oil sources were highlighted. The suppliers of the oil became conscious of the power that they held and soon they used that power to put up the price of oil. The price moved 300 times – mostly up – in the following five years. Countries, industries and companies were taken by complete surprise and forecasts had to be totally rewritten. The days of cycles and trends were over – the age of discontinuity had arrived.

In response to this high level of unpredictability a new approach to planning began to gain popularity. It has come to be known as 'scenario planning'. In essence it works on the premise that 'if you cannot confidently predict the future, then predict a number of futures!'

The scenario planner will take a number of key economic and social (and spiritual) variables, for example, inflation, unemployment, dollar exchange rate, oil price, church giving, church attendance, etc, and combine these to construct a variety of futures. The scenario planner then will choose the 'best guess' future and construct a description of that best guess prediction. In this context, 'best' does not mean 'most attractive', but rather 'most likely on the basis of the data available'. The next step is to take each of the key variables and produce a pessimistic case and optimistic case. For example, the Table 8.6 shows what church attendance in UK might look like in the year 2000.

Three sets of plans can now be prepared – one based on

Pessimistic case	Best guess prediction	Optimistic case
5%	7%	10%

Table 8.6. *Three scenarios for church attendance in the year 2000*

each case. As time goes by figures will become available which will indicate which one of the scenarios is emerging. Thus, whatever future emerges, the organisation is prepared!

The approach can be developed by setting variables against variables. The following example shows how the effects of the Decade of Evangelism might affect the Church and its concern for evangelism and mission in the first decade of the next millennium.

Remember that scenario planning is designed to provide leadership with options. The resultant set of futures is therefore a basis for producing the plan itself.

Preparing the scenarios

The preparation of a set of scenarios is not easily achieved for a subject as complex as the Church and its concern for mission. If we concentrate on the Church and overseas mission it will be simpler. However, whatever the nature of the organisation, the approach is standard, and falls into four major phases:

1. Gathering of information, views and opinions about the future.
2. Analysing and synthesising the gathered information in order to create the set of scenarios of the future.
3. The prayerful selection of the future judged to be the most likely in the light of information and wisdom available.

4. The description of the responses required to best meet the vision of the organisation in the environment envisaged in the future.

The time horizon of a set of scenarios will be chosen to suit the type of organisation and its stage of development. Let us consider the Church and its concern for overseas mission in the first decade of the next century.

1. Gathering information.   I will base this section on my own knowledge and understanding of the Church and mission. For those who wish to carry out their own scenario planning there are some very good writers on the trends in Church and mission, notably Patrick Johnson and Peter Brierley. Gathering data on the future is not easy since most churches and missions would not have plans covering more than five years ahead. Certainly it would be very unusual to come across plans extending beyond a ten year horizon, so the key data will need to be gathered through discussion, reading, listening, prayer and reflection. This first phase is likely to take about six months. My own view of the Church and mission in the post Decade of Evangelism world is shown in summary form in Table 8.7.

2. Analysis.   The major challenge facing the would-be scenario planner is that of drawing together the myriad views, possibilities, trends and pressures in such a manner that a set of consistent and coherent futures can be produced. To aid this process I divide the data into two main categories – the environment and the organisation. This basic division is shown in Figure 8.2.

The two sets can now be sub-divided. This places a structure upon the information and enables a systematic analysis to be completed without too much complexity. The environmental data is divided into five subsets, called 'domains' comprising of the following information:

1. The political environment	3. The spiritual environment a) Home churches
Continuing political instability. Some pro-Western shift. More tribalism and nationalism. Urbanisation. Change, confusion, revolution and deprivation may all be used by God to open minds and hearts. Events in South Africa will influence whole continent. Continuing famine and development needs and opportunities. Islam and Islamic governments growing in strength and in opposition. China as a major world force.	Evangelical growth greater than population growth. Missions increasingly cooperating at home and overseas to reach the unreached peoples. A new sense of expectancy in the Church. Mission takes a higher profile. New mission strategies and structures developed to tackle the unfinished task. New resources to reach the remaining unreached people groups. Reservoir of 'house churches' is released into evangelism and mission. Enormous new input of resources and people released into the work of evangelism and mission.
2. The economic environment	**a) Overseas churches and overseas missions**
Economic failure will cause social unrest and distress. Poverty on the increase. Distribution of wealth internally becoming ever less balanced. Need for rural development crucial but low political priority. Internal communications deteriorating. Developments funded externally likely to be short-lived due to poor maintenance. Political uncertainty likely to discourage foreign investment. Fuel shortages will increase, especially in the Third World, and make operations planning more important. Communication – the strategic technology for the church and mission.	National church growth outstripping church strength. Need for deeper teaching throughout national churches. Need for national churches to become more self-supporting. More national leadership. The need of 'the whole church to the whole world' concept. Need for overall mission strategy within each country will increase. Outreach to Islam and persecution from Islam.

Table 8.7. *Views of the future*

- The political domain
- The economic domain
- The spiritual domain (the Church)
- The technological domain
- The evangelism/mission domain.

Since the data is gathered from many different sources, inevitably there are some widely differing views of the future in the domains. This, at first, may seem unhelpful, but in fact it is very useful since the scenario approach requires that three futures are described:

- a best prediction based on experience.
- an optimistic case based on the more positive trends and opinions.
- a pessimistic case based on the more negative trends and opinions.

The different views enable the three futures to be described for the Church and the world. The domains of 'the Church' and 'The World' are of course interactive. For example changes in the economic environment, particularly unemployment levels, could impact on the Church's resources both negatively – in reduced income – and positively – in making more lay involvement possible.

1. The World Environment

Figure 8.2. *Two sets of data*

The World / Home Church	Improvement	Best prediction	Deterioration
Improvement	1	2	3
Best prediction	4	5	6
Deterioration	7	8	9

Table 8.8. *Nine basic scenarios*

Synthesis. The integration of the two sets of data is obtained by setting the Church and World information into a matrix as shown in Table 8.8.

In this form we now have nine basic scenarios in which number 5 would be our 'Best Prediction', number 1 would be universal improvement and number 9 would be world/Church deterioration on our best prediction. Note that the 'best' prediction might be much worse or much better than the present. In this form the data collected can now be used to describe our best predictions and describe the eight surrounding scenarios in the matrix.

It should be remembered that the aim of the scenario planning technique is to provide a snapshot overview of the world and the Church some ten to fifteen years hence. It is true that 'we know not what a day may bring forth'[19], but it is also true that we may 'see through a glass darkly'.[20] It is this latter capacity that we seek to draw upon while still committing ourselves day by day to the God who directs our path in response to our acknowledgement of and trust in Him.[21]

3. Selecting the future options. In my contacts with churches and missions, my general impression of leaders' views are often encouraging, although the level of awareness within the Church of the need for evangelism and mission is still patchy. In addition, the Church often has a fragmented response to evangelism and mission. However, the general feeling is that both the awareness and the response of the Church to evangelism and mission is moving in the right direction. Given that in the mid 1990s, the spiritual environment and commitment to evangelism and mission is still patchy and fragmented, the options for the Church in the post Decade of Evangelism world are:

- Strong, concerned and involved in evangelism and mission (improvement)

- Fragmented, patchy awareness (best prediction)

- Weak, no vision (deterioration).

The general consensus from my data suggests that over the period under consideration the 'Home Church' will move from the patchy, fragmented scenario to a 'strong, concerned, involved' scenario. I regard this as a change of fundamental significance.

Politically and economically, the world of the mid 1990s is in a state of uncertainty. This is characterised by international tension and unrest, prolonged recession, wide currency exchange fluctuations and a growing gap between the North and South as predicted in the Brandt Report.[22] This uncertainty is still the best prediction for the world of the next ten to fifteen years and the options therefore are:

- Growing stability (improvement).

- Continued uncertainty (best prediction).

- Increased conflict (deterioration).

It is difficult to find counsel which would support a much greater level of stability and certainty in tomorrow's world and, though some views were indeed pessimistic, they were 'worst fears' rather than realistic expectations.

The chosen scenario

Table 8.9 illustrates the type of environment which could be expected under the nine scenarios. The matrix is explained below.

The horizontal headings at the top of the chart show three options for the world situation. The vertical column on the left of the chart shows three options for the Church with regard to evangelism and mission.

The 'Weak, No Vision' situation is where the church itself is weak and has little vision for outreach and for missions in general. The 'Fragmented, Patchy Awareness' situation is one where there is a fragmented and patchy awareness of the need for missions in general. The 'Strong, Concerned, Involved' applies to the situation in which we would hope to see the Church with regard to mission in general.

The nine squares within the matrix give some of the features which could be expected as a result of the conjunction of any of the World and Church situations. The best prediction of the 2010 world scene is 'continued uncertainty', which represents little change from the 1995 situation.

The 1995 scene in the home Church is 'Fragmented, Patchy Awareness' as regards evangelism and mission. The scene by 2100 is expected to be the 'Strong, Concerned, Involved' situation. The 1995 scenario is therefore at the conjunction of 'Continued Uncertainty' in the world, and 'Fragmented, Patchy Awareness' in the home Church.

The 2010 scenario towards which we should be planning is:

- Continued uncertainty in the world political environment, but

The World / The Church and Mission	Growing Stability	Continued Uncertainty	Increased Conflict
Strong, Concerned, Involved	– Growth and continuity – Easier selection and training of mission staff – Fulfilment and satisfaction of mission staff	– Mission work well financed and staffed – Mission able to respond to needs – Sensitive to change – Strong training function	– Need for increased flexibility – Need for more funding – Greater amount of relief work?
Fragmented, Patchy Awareness	– Cost cutting – Selective thrusts toward home churches – Mission to the churches to generate more interest in mission – Building on the Decade of Evangelism	– Need for strong Public Relations – Emphasis on recruitment – Need for mission cooperation across Europe – Need for strong financial and management controls – Stop/go activities	– Recruitment problems – Missed opportunities – Constraints – Increased pressures on church and mission leadership.
Weak, No Vision for mission	– Missions will need to be self supporting – Major reductions in mission staff – Slow, evolutionary development – Need to be highly selective in establishing priorities	– Increased reliance on commercial work – Greater use of 'short termers' – Selective withdrawal of missions – Collapse, breakdown of western world mission as we know it.	– Increased reliance on relief type work – Need to keep experienced staff – Mission merger – Smaller units – Crisis management

Table 8.9. *Nine Scenarios*

– Strong, concerned, involved churches.

This moves the best prediction upward in the matrix to top-centre from the position in the middle-centre. This top-centre scenario I call the 'Good Samaritan Scenario', because it represents strong concern in a troubled world.

The Good Samaritan Scenario

There are four core features associated with this view of the future:

1. Adequate financing and staffing for evangelism and mission which enable an adequate response to local and overseas needs.
2. Continuing contact and liaison at all levels with missions, churches, para-church organisations, governments etc, would enable the Church to develop greater sensitivity to constant changes.
3. A strong training initiative toward evangelism and mission.
4. Integration and cooperation with missions and churches world wide but particularly in Europe.

The Good Samaritan Scenario is indeed one of encouragement and offers much in the way of opportunity and growth but brings with it considerable challenge.

Let me summarise what has been said thus far. Looking forward from the mid 1990s, the scenario approach suggests that by 2010:

– The world will still be in an uncertain, unstable condition, economically and politically.

– The Home Churches in Western Europe will be much more aware of and active in supporting the needs of evangelism and mission.

– Missions will be working much more closely together in

attempts to meet local or area needs overseas in a coordinated manner.

- The needs of the Church worldwide might well be much greater than in 1995, primarily because it will be larger, be suffering more opposition/persecution and in many cases have become more materialistic.

- Communications technology will have changed the way many missions operate.

The most significant changes therefore are those antici-pated in the Home Church and Missions, coupled with significant growth in overseas churches and the potential impact of communications technology.

What do these scenarios mean for the Church? Clearly, although many changes are expected over the following ten years, in essence, the 2010 Good Samaritan scenario anticipates that the Church will:

- Have grown in all aspects of mission.

- Greatly strengthen its outreach to the local, national and international communities.

- Continue to enter into wider cooperation particularly across the pan-evangelical spectrum.

The Strategic Plan

Once the chosen scenario has been described, the next step is to produce a Strategic Plan. What are the implications of the scenario for the Church and how does the Church prepare for the future? These questions are answered using the six part model which is described in detail in Chapter Thirteen. The six parts are

- The Church's identity and public image

- The Church's relationships

- The Church's structures and systems

- The Church's resources

- The Church's tasks and activities

- The Church's people.

Strengths and Weaknesses

The advantages and disadvantages of the scenario approach are set out in Table 8.10.

Advantages	Disadvantages
1. easy to work with 2. flexible 3. readily reflects change 4. long term 5. improves awareness of users	1. lengthy procedures 2. lot of work involved 3. broad brush, no details 4. quantitative data needs a computer to handle effectively.

Table 8.10. *The scenario approach*

The Black Hole of Planning

Planning does not remove the uncertainty of the future, but it does allow you to cope more effectively with whatever future comes. In my book on time management I describe a number of attitudes to planning. The pictures I use there are maritime. There is the Viking planner who simply launches forth hoping that his god is going with him! Then there is the Titanic planner who plans for every possible eventually except what actually happens! Then there is the Polaris planner who plans in secret and the Santa Maria planner who follows the vision and takes his crew with him. Finally there is the Brendan planner – the

6th century Irish monk who first(?) discovered America – he tried seven times before the vision was realised. From these examples we learn that effective planning needs to be short term and long term, flexible, open, based on team work and persistent. But that does not make it any easier. There are still many dangers in planning. But there are even more if we do not plan.

A major tension for churches, missions and Christian organisations emerges when they consider the balance between faith and planning. It is a false comparison. Planning is an act of faith! All plans are simply statements of faith. A plan tells you what you believe will happen and thus every business and every government which prepares a plan engages in acts of faith. This is something that the secular world finds very uncomfortable and difficult to accept. There might be a lot of science in the critical path planning, there might be a lot of accountancy principles in the budget, there might be a lot of complex economics in the forecast, but more than all of these ingredients there is faith. The secular planner is no less a man or woman of faith than the Christian – in fact, because of the unreliability of most planning models you might even say that they were people of greater faith!

Nevertheless, tensions exist for the Christian. Perhaps the greatest dilemma is how much should the plan be based on scientific management practices and how much should it be based on spiritual insight? I would suggest that the short term and the long term should be more dependant on the spiritual dimension, while the medium term should make more use of the logical and rational aspects of our God-given gifts. Figure 8.3 illustrates this.

Figure 8.4 shows the need for balance and the dangers of operating at the extremes. Remember that all planning is an activity of faith; plans are statements of belief. However 'faith by itself, if it is not accompanied by action is dead'[23] and when it comes to planning the 'action' is the action of the mind. Plans which have little thought to them are irrational and a denial of the mental gifts that God has given us. The Irrational Black Hole is the region of pure passion, revelation and vision. Although these are all legitimate and vital in change, without the understanding which comes from thoughtful reflection and without the counting of the cost which comes from planning, they are dangerous experiences.

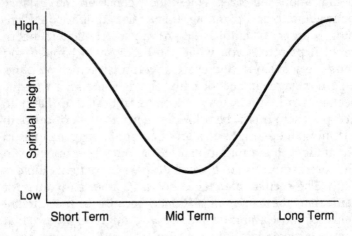

Figure 8.3. *The balance between spiritual and logical planning*

However, pure thought and concentrated mental logic are not the answer, for the Rational Black Hole awaits those who trust solely in their own understanding. Beware of the thinking man who rejects the irrational, intuitive insight; steer clear of the thinking woman who rejects the feelings of the sixth sense, they are both in danger of being drawn into the false security of the totally rational plan. It is a false plan since we do not live among people who are rational, nor do we deal with a rational God! You do not agree? Then please explain what is rational about love!

The Ill-considered Black Hole draws the unthinking

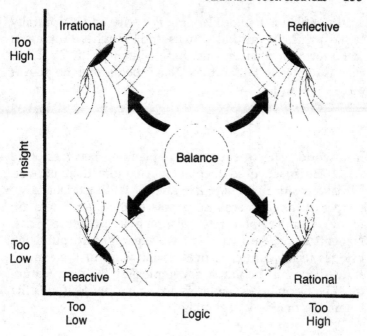

Figure 8.4. *The black holes of spiritual and logical planning*

people who reject insight. These are the 'it will be all right on the night brigade'. They are those who without thought reject planning because it is too much work, although they would not admit this. More likely they would take unthinking comfort from out-of-context scriptures such as 'Do not boast about tomorrow, for you do not know what a day may bring forth,'[24] seeing these as prohibitions on planning rather than exhortations to trust God in all your ways.[25]

The Reflective Black Hole is a kaleidoscope of contradicting insight and logic. It is the trap for the philosophers of this world, a place of endless debate and no action. Beware!

It is in the balance of revelation and logic that the truly

spiritual plan is found. Planning is a wise and scripturally based principle. All individuals and churches do plan in some form or other. As one commentator put it 'To fail to plan is to plan to fail!' A poor plan is better than no plan at all.

Summary

In a world of increasing change, planning becomes more vital. Christians need to plan much more than not-yet-Christians since planning is an act of faith. Christians, as people of the faith are also people of the plan. There are many examples of careful planning in Scripture: Ezra, Nehemiah, St. Paul, etc, and we are called to build the bridges to the future, to prepare the way for the coming King. Plans may be simple or complex but their key feature must be flexibility. The plan is not an end in itself, it is the beginning of a new beginning.

Reflections on of Planning your Changes

1. How could we develop and apply the seven practices of planning in our church or organisation? See Table 8.1 and the seven questions below.

   1.1 How could we become the people of repentance?

   ....

   ....

   1.2 How could we increase our concern for tomorrow's generation?

   ....

   ....

1.3 How could we increase the spiritual dimension in our planning?

....

....

1.4 How could we increase the number of minds involved in our forward thinking?

....

....

1.5 How could we use our plans to increase people's willingness to give their time and their talents to the work of our church or charity?

....

....

1.6 How could we use our plans to increase commitment and involvement?

....

....

1.7 How could we bring prayer and celebration into our planning process?

....

....

2. What scenarios do we base our plans upon? (Do not say 'None!'; every plan is based on some view of the future!)

....

....

3. How could we extend our present planning horizons from say, one year to five years, or from five years to fifteen years?

....

....

References in Chapter Eight

1. Psalm 20:4b.
2. Cormack, David, *Seconds Away!*, Monarch, England, 1991, p 71 – 81.
3. 1 Chronicles 21:18.
4. 1 Chronicles 22:1.
5. Vine, W.E, *Expository Dictionary*, Oliphants, 1970, p 279.
6. Psalm 20:4a.
7. 1 Chronicles 28:2.
8. Revelation 1:8.
9. Revelation 2:11.
10. 1 Chronicles 28:12.
11. 1 Chronicles 28:19.
12. Exodus 3:8.
13. Genesis 6:16.
14. 1 Chronicles 29:2.
15. 1 Chronicles 29:6.
16. Nanus Burt, *Visionary Leadership*, Jossey-Bass Publishers, San Francisco, 1992, p 16.
17. The Cathedral Church of St. Mary the Virgin, Edinburgh, 1990.
18. King Stuart, *Hope has Wings*, Marshall Pickering, 1993, p 297.
19. Proverbs 27:1.
20. St. Paul, 1 Corinthians 13:12.
21. Proverbs 3:6.
22. Brandt, William, *The Brandt Report*.
23. James 2:17.
24. Proverbs 27:1.
25. Proverbs 3:6.

CHAPTER NINE

PACING YOUR CHANGES

How often I have longed to gather your children together, as a hen gathers its chicks under her wings, but you were not willing.[1]

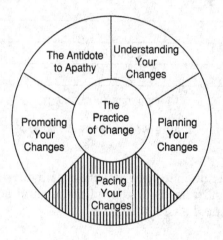

In the last chapter we considered the planning of change, but there are limits to change. Sometimes the prevailing situation is such that the change does not get off the ground. This is a result of a failure to penetrate what I call the 'Apathy Barrier'. On the other hand some changes fail because they produce a life-threatening situation. This I term the 'Crisis Ceiling'.

Figure 9.1 represents the limits to change. The leaders of the change need to raise the level of interest and commit-

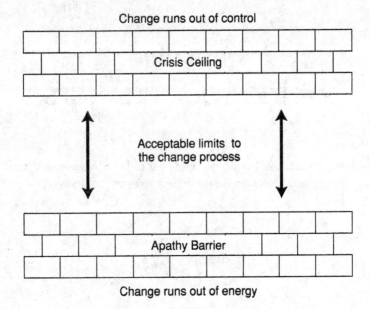

Figure 9.1 *The limits to change*

ment high enough to penetrate the Apathy Barrier. But, the leadership also needs to control the level of activity such that it avoids the Crisis Ceiling.

The Apathy Barrier

The emergence of AIDS among the homosexual communities of the Western world represented a classic case of apathy in the face of devastating change. At first there was a denial of the condition, then a rejection of any links between the condition and the deviant sexual practices, then a refusal to modify these practices when the transmission mechanisms were eventually established. Finally, as a result of transfer of the virus to the heterosexual community, the homosexuals were able to point to AIDS as having nothing really to do with them – it was a general problem.

To overcome the apathy barrier or the 'We-do-not-need-this-change, things-are-OK-as-they-are' syndrome requires us to take a number of specific initiatives. First, the problems of the current practice must be high-lighted. As long as people are content with the way things are done at the moment, then they will not be inclined to strive for improvements or change. We can see this clearly in the experience of the prophet Haggai. The people had become comfortable, their houses had been rebuilt, things were not too bad,[2] so no further progress was seen as necessary. The acceptable had become the enemy of the possible. It was only when the prophet entered the scene and stirred up the discontent by pointing out all the social problems[3] – inflation, agricultural inefficiency, inadequate storage facilities, poor quality food and wine, etc – that the people were moved to change.

The second step must be to give the people a vision for change. That vision must be attractive, inspiring and owned by everyone. Without a clear vision to arouse people's achievement motivation they will not move forward. The prophet's message provided not only a short-term vision of a rebuilt House of God,[4] but a long term vision of that house becoming the centre of worldwide worship.[5] The third initiative must be the indication of an easy way forward. Those required to change must be asked to take small, simple initial steps. The first action required must be without too much risk of failure. Once again Haggai gave simple steps: 'All you have to do is go up to the hills and cut a few trees.'[6]

Finally, the cost of change must be addressed. All change brings with it some cost. To move forward means to leave something or someone behind. The cost of change, the cost of moving forward, must be less than the cost of staying where you are.

Discontent, vision, simple first steps and an affordable cost are necessary to overcome the apathy barrier. Given these four conditions you can expect to avoid any change initiative grinding to a premature halt. One way to express the relationships between the four conditions is to put these into a little formula called the *Apathy Barrier Formula*:

$$C = f(D.V.F) > £.$$

Where change (C) is a function (f) of the level of discontent (D), the clarity of the common vision (V) and the simplicity of the first steps (F) being greater than (>) the cost of change (£).

Too little change can kill. Without the stimulus of change, without the threat of change, organisations can die from lack of creativity. The list of closed businesses and churches is endless and almost all because they could not change fast enough. True, there is risk in too much change, but life does not come with a risk-free guarantee! There is always a cost and of course the cost of changing is never ever simply financial.

The Crisis Ceiling

Apathy is dangerous, but revolution could prove fatal. Change produces stress and too much change can produce too much stress, the stress produces strain and the strain leads to crisis. Organisational and personal stress are proportional to five key variables.

First, the *speed of change* – move too fast and you have crisis because neither individuals nor organisation can cope with the stresses involved. In the Exodus story the liberation was a discontinuity. One day they were slaves the next day they were free. But they had not learned to act as free men and women. At the first sign of difficulty they were thrown into confusion as they faced the Red Sea with the Egyptian armies at their heels.[6]

Lesson One – Do not be afraid of going slowly, only of standing still.

The second variable is the *shift of direction*. Those organisations which have been open to change for a number of years will find change easy to embrace, while those for whom change is a new concept may struggle. After forty years of uncertainty and change in their wilderness journeying, the Israelites were ready for anything. Their first target was Jericho,[7] possibly the most fortified and dangerous of cities in the Promised Land. Forty years before, the thought of having to go to war at all created one of the greatest crises of Moses' leadership.[8] Time is needed to get used to the idea of change.

Lesson Two – Avoid U-turns.

The third variable is the *degree of control* over the speed, direction and content of the change. The more the initiative can be controlled by the individual or the team, the greater the speed of change that can be accommodated.

Lesson Three – Imposition creates Resistance.

I spend several weeks each year in the Third World, visiting mission and relief organisations. To cope with the pressures of so much travel, I try to ensure that I take plenty of exercise. Consider how I would feel in the following situations. Towelling down after a swim, I decide that its time to lose a bit of weight – at my time of life it is easy to eat more that I need and to exercise less than I should – so I decide to cut out sugar and potatoes for a couple of months. I am in control of the changes in diet which I plan, so I feel OK. The next week I happen to be visiting the doctor to top up my various injections prior to a tropical trip. 'David,' says the doctor, 'You seem to be a bit overweight: step on the scales and, while we are at it, let me take your blood pressure.' As a result of the visit I come out with a rigorous diet which says no sugar and no

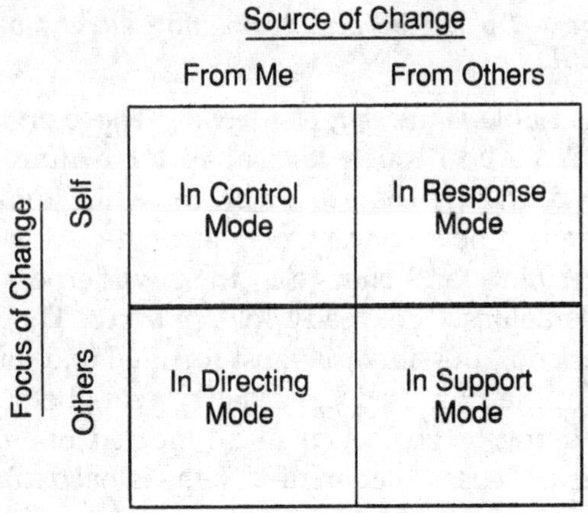

Source of Change

Figure 9.2 *Change and control*

potatoes for a couple of months. How do I feel about it? Very different! I am no longer in control, the doctor is setting the pace. He is in control and although the diet is the same as the one I chose for myself, I now feel very much less positive about the change. Giving as much control as you can to the people – and then a bit more – enables them to respond much more positively to change. Figure 9.2 captures the essence of the concept of change and control.

As long as I am in the 'From Me' situations then I remain in control whether the focus of the change is on self or others. When the change is initiated by others, then I tend to fall back into the defensive mode when the focus of change is self. When the source of the change is others and the focus of change is on others, then I have the opportunity of supporting those in change.

> **Lesson Four – Give as much control over the change as you can to others.**

A further variable is the *information available* about the progress and future direction of the initiative. People can cope with more change if they are kept informed. Throughout the wilderness journey the Children of Israel had to be kept informed and reminded of their progress. They needed the perspective of the past and the future in order to cope with the pressures of the day to day.[9]

Lesson Five – Remember the three C's of successful change: Communicate! Communicate! and Communicate!

Finally, the greater the *belief* in the proposed change and the level of commitment to it, the faster people will be prepared to move toward it. They will also endure greater uncertainty, stress and pressure arising from change. To quote one change master:

> The first phase of change is developing conviction . . . The second phase is commitment . . . The third phase is conversion.[10]

These five variables form the Crisis Ceiling and can be brought together in a second formula called the *Crisis Ceiling Formula*:

$$Cr = f(Sp.Sd.Dc.In.) > B$$

Where crisis (Cr) is a function (f) of the speed of change (Sp), the shift of direction (Sd), the degree of control (Dc), the information available (In) all being more than my belief (B) in my ability to cope with the change.

Of course when it comes to change, we have to beware of the formulae, because that can change too! Success in a changing world has to do with how well we learn to change, not how well we learn the formulae!

Learning

Change is about learning. Those at the frontiers of change must be prepared to experience the unknown and communicate the lessons of that experience to others.

Most organisations have no formal methods of learning other than financial, departmental and personal goal-setting and review. These are inadequate for managing major change since they are all subordinate to and influenced by the changes taking place. In addition to this difficulty, each organisation – church, mission or business – has developed its own learning style and so tends to learn in a biased way depending on its culture.

The way organisations learn depends on four factors – the leadership style, which may be participative or directive, the communication flow, which may be top down or free flow, the management focus, which may be backward or forward and the attitude to success and failure, which may be to blame others or to take ownership of the outcome and the learning.

The orientation to each of these factors will determine whether an organisation learns and grows from its experiences or simply keeps records of its experiences. The following questionnaire will enable you to determine whether you are making the most of your organisation's learning potential.

Please score yourself according to the following code in the learning questionnaire:

> 5 points, definitely agree
>
> 4 points, mostly agree
>
> 3 points, tend to agree
>
> 2 points, tend to disagree
>
> 1 point, mostly disagree
>
> 0 definitely disagree.

What is your total score? The higher the score the greater the risk to your organisation of failing to learn effectively. Now place your scores in Table 9.1 to identify the main risks that you face. If you scored more than 10 in any of the sub totals, some action is needed in these areas.

Learning Questionnaire

Please consider your church, mission or organisation as a whole and score it 0 to 5 in respect of the following descriptions.

Score

☐ 1. We take our identity from what we do rather than who we are.

☐ 2. People are status conscious in our organisation.

☐ 3. We are highly compartmentalised.

☐ 4. When things go wrong we blame someone.

☐ 5. Most of our problems are due to the environment in which we have to operate.

☐ 6. Our failures are due to the enemy 'out there'.

☐ 7. Our problems are caused by people outside the organisation.

☐ 8. Long term plans take the uncertainty out of life.

☐ 9. Being proactive helps us keep ahead.

☐10. We tend to be event driven.

☐11. We are highly reactive.

☐12. We tend to focus on the 'what' rather then the 'how' of change.

☐13. Changes in our world take us by surprise.

☐14. Longer term trends do not interest us as much as today's opportunities.

☐15. We have very little time for reflection.

☐16. We are reluctant to learn from our mistakes.

☐17. We never apply the learning from one experience to another.

☐18. We are reluctant to examine failures for lessons.

☐19. We talk teamwork but never work as a team.

☐20. Inter-departmental cooperation is low.

☐21. Communication is poor.

Sub-totals from statement scores	Risk Faced
1, 2 and 3	Regarding yourself and others in terms of their positions in the organisation, and taking your identity from what you do rather than who you are. This can lead to rigidity and inflexibility.
4, 5 and 6	Projecting the reasons for your church's pain into the outside world. 'The enemy is out there.' This can lead to an unwillingness to address internal problems.
7, 8 and 9	Confusing the preparation of a vision, a mission and goals with 'taking charge'. Vision statements, missions, goals and plans are all statements of faith. They will help you cope better with tomorrow, but they do not take away the need to learn and change. This can lead to a Titanic-like sense of invulnerability.
10, 11 and 12	Becoming focused on what you do rather than how you do it. Management of change requires the what and the how to be leadership's concern. This can lead to becoming very good at the wrong activities.
13, 14 and 15	Failure to spot the creeping threat. 'It is a bit chillier today,' as one mammoth said to another.
16, 17 and 18	Failure to recognise that learning from experience is often an illusion since the consequences of our decisions are often a long time in surfacing – too long for effective change management and too late for learning.
19, 20 and 21	Relying on ideals rather than dealing with things as they are, eg. trying to run as a team when you are nothing like a team – yet. The risk here is that you deny what you are and believe what you are not.

Table 9.1. *Barriers to learning*

For more information on the learning organisation see, *The Fifth Discipline*, by Peter M. Senge.[11]

The Choices

Let us apply some learning to the speed of change. What lessons are there around for us? What are the options? The main decision in implementing change is 'How fast to go?' There are two extremes – evolution or revolution. Do you go for a rapid implementation process or a protracted one? Rapid, man-made change which transforms ourselves or our environments I will call revolutionary change. As one expert in the subject put it:

> A revolution is not a dinner party . . . it cannot be so refined, so leisurely and gentle . . . a revolution is an insurrection, an act of violence.[12]

Revolutions are hard to cope with and are hard to manage successfully. Like catastrophes, they are a shock to the system. They are acts of violence and they are often accompanied by aggression and insurrection. Although they may begin as small and apparently insignificant changes their impact rapidly grows. Revolutions bring resentment and with that comes conflict.

Revolutions can be political as in Eastern Europe of the late 1980s; they can be social as in the response to the AIDS epidemic; they can be spiritual as in the great movements of the Holy Spirit throughout the centuries; they can be personal as in an individual's commitment to new ways of life and behaviour. Whatever their focus, revolutions are here to stay! Tom Peters says:

> Change and constant improvement, the watchwords of the 1980s, are no longer enough. Not even close. Only revolution, and perpetual revolution at that, will do.[13]

Table 9.2 sets out the advantages and disadvantages of the two options. Sometimes we have no choice. We simply have to react as quickly as possible to a change over which we have no control. However, it is also a matter of culture. Some cultures are more comfortable with evolution, others prefer revolution.

> Active mutators in placid and stable times tend to die off. They are selected against. Reluctant mutators in quickly changing times are also selected against.[14]

Evolutionary change is imperceptibly slow. Mutation is vital for survival in a changing world but for many muta-

Feature	Evolution	Revolution
Characteristics	Slow Paced Gradual Phased	Rapid Forced Sudden Cathartic
Risks	Too slow for survival. Creates casualties – evolution has killed off more creatures than revolution!	Too fast. Strong reaction. High levels of conflict. Pockets of resistance. High level of casualties.
Benefits	Gives time to adapt. Training can take place. Adjustments can be made gradually.	Gives very clear message – 'Change or perish!' Creates enthusiasm. Can give competitive advantage.

Table 9.2. *Implementation options*

tion is a slow process. This may seem much more comfortable but there is a message for us from evolution:

Thinking Horizons

Table 9.3 shows the different thinking horizons of some national cultures. The greater the thinking horizon the more evolutionary the change can be. These figures come from research carried out by the European Management Research Institute. Forty countries were compared according to how far ahead their management cultures planned. The average Japanese company, for example was found to plan twice as far ahead as the average Greek company and 60% more than the average UK company.

Most churches plan on an annual basis using their budgets as the key planning tool. The Decade of Evangelism has had a significant effect on church planning, pushing the horizons out beyond three years for many parishes for the first time. Similarly the advent of the new millennium has provided a spur to longer-term planning. However, simply to prepare a plan and select a process is no guar-

Country	Rank
Japan	1
West Germany	3
Finland	5
Norway	8
Netherlands	10
France	12
United States	19
United Kingdom	22
Hong Kong	28
Greece	31

Table 9.3. *National thinking horizons*

antee that you will be able to deliver the plan or stick with the process.

Theory versus Practice

Table 9.4 shows the difference between what one group of UK managers SAID they wanted and how they actually behaved during a major reorganisation. They wanted to follow an evolutionary route and produced a plan based on the characteristics shown in the first column of Table 9.4. What actually happened – in retrospect – is shown in the second column!

Now these leaders were experienced, international managers. There was no question regarding their business skills. They were the best. Yet they did not behave in the way they intended. Why was this? On reflection they recognised that their values of independent action, business results before people's feelings and the importance of competitive advantage had dominated their actual behaviour rather then the value of cooperative team work which had dominated the planning process. Nevertheless, all was not lost. The shift from planned evolution to actual revolution provided the leadership team with the opportunity to learn. The lessons that they identified as a result of their experiences have been noted.

Tom Peters recommends that we delete the word 'change' from our vocabulary and replace it with 'revolution'. Change is too stable a word to describe what is going on in our world![15]

Desired Change (Evolution)	Actual Change (Revolution)
1. Take time to build a common vision of the future.	Conflict developed between the business needs and the people's needs. The business could not wait until a common vision was in place.
2. Agree the underlying goals of change and communicate these to everyone affected.	Leadership effort had focused on gaining acceptance of the new organisation rather than explaining the rationale behind the changes.
3. Achieve the changes in a planned manner, following an agreed strategy.	Limited discussion on the plan resulted in departments going their own way.
4. Agree and follow a consistent leadership approach to managing the changes.	Inconsistency abounded due to the mixed quality of consultation down the line.
5. Gain understanding and commitment of all staff to the changes.	Consultation inhibited by constraints of confidentiality.
6. Implement the changes in a consistent manner particularly in relation to personnel matters.	Very little cohesion in the way personnel matters were handled.
7. Review progress regularly and build the capacity to manage change based on experience and learning.	Review meetings were planned but cancelled.

Table 9.4. *Theory versus reality*

Lessons From a Revolutionary Change

1. Revolution brings resentment
2. Management energy goes into reducing guilt
3. Different leadership approaches emerge
4. Managers privately seek ways forward
5. Fragmentation occurs
6. Change planning becomes a priority
7. Review meetings can be a basis for co-ordination
8. Learning begins to surface after success and progress
9. Revolutions are not always 'bad things'

Reflections on Pacing Your Changes

1. Look back to the Apathy Formula. What is preventing change in your church or organisation at the moment?

....

....

....

....

....

2. How much stress are you currently experiencing because of change? Examine the Crisis Formula. What could be done to reduce the level of stress in your church or organisation?

....

....

....

....

....

3. Look back to Table 9.1. What are the risks to your church or organisation because you are not learning? What could be done to reduce the risks?

....

....

....

....

....

References in Chapter Nine

1. St. Luke 13:34.
2. Haggai 1:2.
3. Haggai 2:9.
4. Haggai 1:8.
5. Haggai 1:5.
6. Exodus 14:10.
7. Joshua 2:1.
8. Numbers 14:4.
9. Leviticus 26:13.
10. Crosby, Philip, Let's Talk Quality, McGraw-Hill, 1989, pp. 15, 16.
11. Senge, Peter, The Fifth Discipline, Century Business, London, 1993.
12. Mao Tse-tung, An Investigation into the Peasant Movement in Hunan, in Selected Works, Vol. 4, Foreign Language Press, Peking 1972, p. 28.
13. Peters, Tom, The Tom Peters Seminar, Macmillan, London 1994, p. 271.
14. Sagan and Druyan, Shadows of our Forgotten Ancestors, Random House, New York, 1992, p.87.
15. Peters, Tom, The Tom Peters Seminar, Macmillan, London, 1994.

CHAPTER TEN

PROMOTING YOUR CHANGES

He that complies against his will is of his own opinion still.[1]

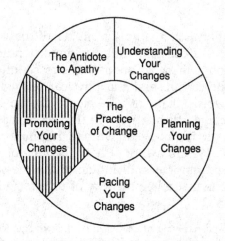

Good communication is crucial during times of change. Unfortunately, throughout history people have had problems with communication. George Eliot said 'The people of the world are islands shouting at each other across a sea of misunderstanding.'[2]

The problem is not simply one of different languages. One commentator suggests that 'English is the common language that divides Britain and America!'.[3] So how we use our own language is often a source of misunderstanding. Consider this sentence 'I hope you are not driving my car to that party on Saturday night!' How many different ways could you emphasise the words? There are at least ten different interpretations possible based on which word is emphasised. But even when we use the same words and use the same meaning and place the same emphasis on the words, often we have difficulty in getting the message across. In this chapter we will explore some of the reasons for those difficulties and provide some tools to overcome the resistance that leaders experience in periods of change.

Communication

Communication is not simply a matter of the words that we use. Our self concepts and our understanding of our role in relation to those we are trying to reach influence our message. Our culture and the physical setting will also colour the words that we use. Hence the message that eventually comes through to the hearer is loaded with ambiguities. 'It is not what we say, it's how we say it that matters'. We are aware of how the tone of voice, the inflections and emphasis all influence the message. John Adair suggests that a helpful way of understanding communication is:

> The giving and receiving of shared ideas, knowledge, feelings – the contents of the mind, heart and spirit of man – by such means as speech, writing or signs.[4]

At the heart of this concept of communication is the idea of sharing. Adair's idea helps emphasise the two-way nature of communication – it is giving and receiving by whatever means. It is a two-way process. The greatest danger is that we reduce our communication during periods of change rather than increase it. Perhaps we think that the less people know the less they have to object against. But people do not need facts to object, they are quite happy to object against fiction and rumour!

The Function of Communication in Change

Communication is the life-blood of change. Communication enables the organisation to operate as one unit during the inevitable unsettling effects of change. Communication serves five main functions[5] during change as shown in Figure 10.1. These five functions of communication are vital in periods of change since they help:

1. To maintain the sense of common vision, purpose and direction.
2. To enable all the change initiatives to be done in an orderly and integrated fashion.
3. To maintain the relationships and harmony of the various individuals and departments.
4. To enable effective problem solving and decision making through frequent, regular feedback.
5. Give a sense of confidence and control.[5]

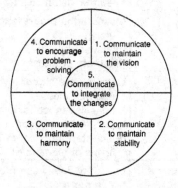

Figure 10.1. *Five functions of communication in periods of change*

Although communication takes time, it saves time. With effective communication, delegation can take place and people can implement changes in their own area with confidence. Mistakes are reduced and control is improved, and of course when change is needed, people will respond more readily if they are kept well informed. Conflict is less likely when the facts, feelings and common vision are readily accessible.

Improving Communication in Times of Change

There are two main strategies for improving communication – first, improve and increase the flow of the communication from the source, and second, remove or reduce the barriers, levels, layers and blockages between the source and the focus of communication. Table 10.1 summarises

Function of communication	Ideas to aid communication
1. Maintaining the common vision	Keep the need for change always in people's minds Focus attention on tomorrow Keep the vision visible
2. Maintaining the stability	Measure the progress towards the vision Review regularly Celebrate progress
3. Maintaining the harmony	Demonstrate higher levels of trust and openness Emphasise those features which people have in common Build inter-dependency and higher levels of team spirit
4. Communicate to encourage problem-solving	Ensure two-way communication flow Listen more Increase the amount of positive feedback
5. Integrating the change activities	Increase the level of co-ordination Provide more opportunity to meet in teams Increase profile of leadership

Table 10.1. *Aids to improved communication*

ways of developing the functions of communication during periods of change.

Targeting Your Communication

Not everyone needs to know everything all of the time, but how many people need to know most things most of the time and who are they? And what about those people who want to know everything but should not? Figure 10.2 is a very helpful guide in this context.

There are three levels of information gatherers – The Headline Readers, The Caption Readers and The Fine Print Readers. Headline Readers rarely buy a newspaper. They are content with the quick glance over someone else's shoulder! The Caption Readers look for a bit more information. They find it in the pictures and the one line captions describing the photographs and illustrations. For the Caption Readers, buying a newspaper is a waste of time, but they are happy to pick one up if they find one left on the train! For these people written summaries are all that they need to keep them happy, perhaps also a poster or two – providing the letters are large and the message is short!

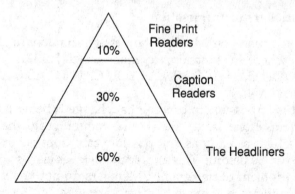

Figure 10.2. *The communication pyramid*

The Fine Print Readers represent those with newsprint ink for blood! They read everything – editorials, articles, reports, reviews, adverts, job vacancies, personal columns, births, deaths and marriages, sports pages, crossword clues and cartoons! These are the 10% of the people who need to be well-informed most of the time. These people are likely to be at the informal, social heart of the organisation and will be the social networkers of the community.

That leaves 90% and of these 60% are the Headline Readers, they are not really interested and don't care whether they know or not about most things. The Caption Readers form the remaining 30% and as we have seen they enjoy a bit more background information, but only from time to time, once a year at the annual general meeting or quarterly at the very most. It is of course important to identify those who have greater or lesser need for more information. Caption Readers and Headliners should not be overlooked.

Every organisation has its problems with communication. Which is the problem group in your organisation? Is it the 'ignorant mass' or the 'knowledgeable few' that you need to reach more effectively?

Disclosure of Information

As you plan your changes, how much should you tell who and when? In summary, experience says 'TELL AS MUCH AS YOU CAN AS SOON AS YOU CAN TO AS MANY AS YOU CAN!'

It is impossible to conceal that change is being planned. Organisations leak! You should communicate the broad objectives as early as you possibly can. Constructive leakage can be helpful. This approach however leaves you with the problem of uncertainty. Members do not know if and when they are going to be affected or whether the pending change is likely to impact on other plans they are making.

However, on balance, the danger of trying to keep things confidential is usually outweighed by the danger of leaks causing gossip, rumour and distortion.

People will feel threatened if they are aware that change is being planned but don't understand what it is about or why it is being considered. A prolonged period of uninformed discussion when people are aware that 'something is going on', can lead to:

a) polarisation of views for and against the feared-for changes;
b) prolonged concern of individuals about the possible negative impact of the change on them personally;
c) team leaders needing to handle high levels of uncertainty in their own group;
d) deterioration in relationships between groups resulting in defensive posturing and much time wasting.

Where an inner group knows what is happening but others do not, then you can expect people to feel manipulated if they believe more things could be revealed. This in turn will lead to a trust gap developing when the members sense that the leadership is in the know but not telling them all there is to know. Team leaders not in the know will have to manage their own uncertainty and their own team's rumours and speculations whilst striving for business as normal. Team leaders in the know will experience inner tension between the loyalty to the leadership which calls for secrecy and loyalty to the team which requires openness.

Consultation Prior to Change

The level of consultation that you use as you contemplate change will be dependant on the nature of the change, the maturity of the group and your style of leadership. Congregational systems should consult more than other systems. However, in general you should consult whenever and wherever possible. The content of the consultation can range from whether or not we change at all, to when a particular phase of the change should be introduced. Remember the value of giving as much control to the people as you can. If you intend to have a change make it clear you are going to make a decision. In this case it must be made clear that the consultation is limited to the content of the change and not whether or not one takes place. Whatever your approach the opinion-formers – the Fine Print Readers – the conservative progressives – must be involved early.

Decide on the degree of involvement of those affected in diagnosing the need for change and planning the implementation of the change. Who are the right people to be involved in the discussion? Think through the consequences of involving or not involving people on the fringes. This depends on the situation, particularly the time pressures and urgency involved.

If you do not consult you need a good reason for not consulting and be ready to take into account the obvious consequences – greater resistance, disruptive conflict, opting out and even resignations from the organisation.

If you make a unilateral leadership decision to change, you need to explain why the change is happening, what is happening and how much further there is to go.

Preparation and Implementation

Leaders often have unrealistic expectations on how quickly changes can be implemented. You must give the people who will be responsible for implementing the change sufficient time to question the rationale for the change and time to think through their feelings, attitudes and reactions to the change proposals. They too need to be clear whether they are going to communicate or consult with their teams. There must be time to help people through their shock and resistance. Team leaders must be clear about whether the proposals are to be communicated in broad outline or final detail. What is open for negotiation? Thorough thinking and thrashing out of detail may be essential to gain unified commitment amongst those who will finally operate in the new situation.

A proposed checklist for the leadership's initial and on going communication in times of change is shown on page 186. Remember, we must not be afraid of moving slowly, only be afraid of standing still. It is a misreading of scripture to believe that we should 'Stand firm and see the deliverance of the Lord.' Moses is immediately rebuked for such sentiments, 'Tell the Israelites to move on.'[6]

Here are some general guidelines for promoting change in others through your own behaviour.

Promoting Change: Guidelines
1. Make your own reasoning explicit, i.e. say how you have arrived at your view and the 'data' upon which it is based.
2. Encourage others to explore your view, e.g. 'Do you see gaps in my reasoning?'
3. Encourage others to provide different views, e.g. 'Do you have either different data or different conclusions, or both?'
4. Actively inquire into others' views that differ from your own, e.g. 'What are your views?' 'How did you arrive at your views?' 'Are you taking into account data that are different from what I have considered?'

Transition

Changes must be monitored throughout their implementation and beyond. Most major changes in organisations take

Leadership's communication checklist

1. Is the vision crisp and concise? Make certain that strategies, tactics, etc are communicated quickly with discipline and care.

2. Are all the team leaders involved? The team leaders should participate with you in the presentation of the change plan to all their people. It is an important presentation, and rehearsal is a must.

3. Have you agreed a list of goals with your team leaders (long-term and short-term goals) based on what they need to focus on during the change period?

4. How will you make certain that the team leaders are and remain the champions of their respective team goals? Their job is just beginning.

5. How will you keep personally involved with monitoring the expected results?

6. Have you developed a professionally printed version of the vision and mission statements for broad distribution?

7. Have you written a short article for the newsletter on your own views of each element of the mission statement?

8. How will you communicate the change plan for future new members? What about a video or taped message?

9. Have you established some small discussion groups for direct feedback and to achieve a higher level of commitment to monitoring progress?

10. How can you use the vision statement as the basis for your own appraisal?

3 to 5 years to be fully bedded into the systems and culture! This extended time period usually comes as a shock to most people, but it explains why we have so much difficulty implementing new ideas. We are too impatient, transitions take time – a long time.

Figure 10.3 shows the typical transition curve. This describes four phases which individuals and organisations experience as they implement major change.

There are four psychological phases to personal transition. The time people stay in a particular phase and the intensity of it for them will vary, but for major organisational and personal changes a minimum period of eighteen months must be expected before long-term adaptation begins. The reason for this protracted period is that the people will continue to be faced with the challenges of unfamiliar tasks and situations with no familiar reference points for at least one year after the introduction of the change. These challenges frequently reduce personal confidence levels. Once a full year has been experienced in the new situation then confidence may begin to return, but this is not guaranteed as reference to the four psychological phases will show.

Phase 1. Shock – Despair or Elation

With the arrival of the change the individual will sense a threat to their world and their traditional ways of doing things. They may feel overwhelmed by the prospect of the changes and may experience varying degrees of panic, anxiety or helplessness. They may show signs of being disoriented and be unable to plan or reason or even understand the situation.

However, the first phase is a phase of extremes. The person may swing from despair to elation quite rapidly in the initial period. But usually the mood swings will

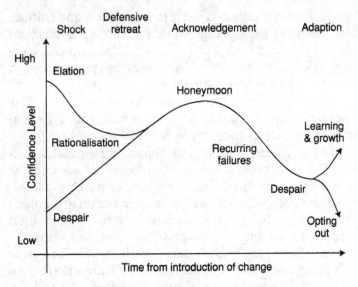

Figure 10.3 *The transition curve*

diminish and stabilise. 'Things were not as bad as we feared' or 'Things were not as good as we hoped.'

Phase 2. Defensive Retreat

Once the individuals have begun to come to terms with the immediate situation, there follows a period of rationalisation. Successes are attributed to personal competence and failures are attributed to 'factors beyond our control'. (See also the blocks to learning page 168.) At this stage the individuals will begin to defend themselves against the threats of failure. This is usually done by attempting to avoid the new reality. There will be a tendency to cling to the old reality and deny or repress the existence of the new situation.

During this period people will be faced constantly with new challenges. How do we cross the Red Sea? How will we feed ourselves? How will we get fresh water? etc, etc.

The constant reminders of their inability to act with confidence and competence tend to have a very depressing effect, forcing them to look hard and long at themselves.

Phase 3. Acknowledgement

During this phase the new reality starts to dawn as the facts of the situation 'impose' themselves on the people. Their defences are broken down and they have to give up their old perspective of reality. They may go through a phase of 'mourning' for the way things were in the old days. They are likely to experience some depression and display apathy or aggression. There are two ways out of this situation – face it and learn how to operate in the new world, or deny it and opt out.

Phase 4. Adaptation

The individuals will eventually start to develop new patterns for coping with or managing the new situation. This will involve testing what it means to survive in the new world. They will start to mobilise their personal and collective resources to deal with the new situation. As they become more successful at dealing with the new world they will experience increasing satisfaction with the new state of affairs and their anxiety will gradually be lowered and their confidence levels return. Of course the alternative adaptation strategy is to quit – quit the job, quit the marriage, quit the mission, quit the church. In extreme situations the despair may lead to suicide – the ultimate quit.

If people are not adjusting to the change it is necessary to identify where they are in this four-phase cycle. You need to decide whether anything can be done to help these people through a phase more quickly, or alternatively, whether more time is needed to come to terms with the change. You can then adjust your plans accordingly.

Categories of Reaction

Most people have a negative psychological response to change, whether or not they see the outcomes as positive or negative. There are five classic reactions which you will encounter.

1. *A fear of failure.* We draw back, we avoid taking risks, we settle for less in order to avoid the pain of failing. Therefore we revise the goals downwards – 'Go ye into as much of the world as you think you can cope with.'
2. *Over-certainty.* We are rigid in our problem-solving responses. We judge on the basis of our stereotypes. We don't check out the assumptions we make about people and situations. Therefore we restrict our responses to the tried and tested ways – 'Go ye into those parts of the world that you have always gone into and do what you have always done.'
3. *Fear of the unknown.* We avoid situations which lack clarity or which have an unknown or low probability of success. We need to know the future before going forward. Therefore we become over-cautious and delay action – 'Tarry ye at Jerusalem until ye receive the power of the Holy Spirit, Mercator's Projection, Geosatellite Positioning, The Information Super-Highway and Tom Pearce's old grey mare.'
4. *Need for balance.* We are unable to tolerate disorder, confusion or ambiguity. We dislike complexity. We have excessive need for order and symmetry. Therefore we do not consider anything which may rock the boat or cause conflict. 'Begin at Jerusalem, Judea and Samaria – if that is OK with the Samaritans.'
5. *Commitment to the present.* We have helped to create the present and have too high a stake in the status quo to think that there can be a better future. 'Begin at

Jerusalem and go back to the mount of transfiguration
– it was great there!'

These psychological reactions to change occur because the
people are passing through a personal period of instability
and in this context a positive change can be as stressful as a
negative one. So, for example, promotion in the job can be
as disorienting as demotion, although neither may be as
traumatic as losing one's job.

People will move through their transitional phases with
more or less speed and with different degrees of difficulty,
but they will all pass through them in some way. In the
early phases of personal transition people are likely to
resist change because they seek stability and security. A
common feature of organisational transition is high uncertainty and low stability. Thus the needs of an individual
are not normally met in the course of an organisation
change, unless you take steps to deal with the fear that
change so often brings. One of the steps to reduce fear is to
make use of open and regular reviews of progress.

Reviews

Reviews should concern themselves with ensuring that:

1. The aim of the change has been realised.
2. The relationships have been strengthened by the
   change.
3. The supporting systems and structures and procedures
   are compatible with the change.
4. The resources, in terms of skills, people, technology,
   budgets, etc are consistent with the new situation.
5. The new activities are consistent with the vision.
6. The personal commitment and motivation of the members have been strengthened.

There are three types of review which are commonly used by organisations. These are:

o the Static Review
o the Dynamic Review
o the Organic Review

The *Static Review* is the most common approach. It is useful for all those who want to be wise after the event! It is an essential tool in the exact science of hindsight! There are a lot of people who are just waiting to tell you what you ought to have done! Static Reviews are like postmortems. It might be very interesting to know that the minister died of a heart attack brought on by overwork, lack of holidays, lack of support, poor salary, inadequate housing and the unreasonable expectations of the congregation. Interesting? Yes! But helpful to the minister? No! Much more useful for the dead leader and family would have been the Dynamic Review.

The *Dynamic Review* recognises that in order to live you have to learn. It sees change as being a series of steps and each step must be reviewed in order to feed the learning back into the plans for the next step. Thus, in our ministerial example at the very least the lessons from the postmortem will be applied to the next vicar. Much better would be to review the situation annually and ensure that the lessons are built on year by year in a dynamic way.

The *Organic Review* does not wait until the year is over before it feeds back the learning. The Organic Review utilises the learning on a continuous basis. Consider a room temperature control, it is a dynamic review mechanism. You set the thermostat at a chosen temperature and the heating is controlled around that. However, an organic approach to room temperature control would recognise that you were too hot or too cold and change the setting on the thermostat. This is the way that changes should be

The Static Review

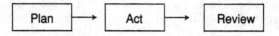

The Dynamic Review

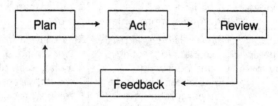

The Organic Review

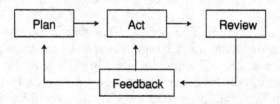

Figure 10.4. *Types of review*

reviewed – on an organic, ongoing basis. Figure 10.4 shows the three types.

The strengths and weaknesses of the three approaches are shown in Table 10.2.

Content of a Review

What should be reviewed? What should be reviewed is not simply what is being done but also how it is being done and its impact on the many parts of the organisation.

Figure 10.5 shows a useful outline for the content of an

Type	Strengths	Weaknesses
The Static Review	Fast Simple Safe	The game is over so nothing can be done Post mortem Not so safe after all!
The Dynamic Review	Focuses on learning Enables future plans to be improved Promotes improvement	Danger of focusing on what did not work rather than what did work
The Organic Review	Review is integral part of planning, acting and reviewing Enables learning to be incorporated into current action Minimises failure	May distract from the work in hand May fail to emphasise the importance of the review process.

Table 10.2. *Strengths and weaknesses of reviews*

organisation change review. This should be used in conjunction with the Change Review Questionnaire which follows. The Change Review Questionnaire enables the positive and negative aspects of the change to be identified. The eight point framework in Figure 10.5 was used in Chapter Eight for the planning of an organisation strategy and is also used in Chapter Thirteen for the analysis of a diocese.

The Change Review Questionnaire

This questionnaire has been designed for use six to eighteen months after the introduction of a major change. At least one third of the members of the church, mission or organisation should be given the opportunity to complete the questionnaire. Returned questionnaires should be treated as 'confidential', although a summary of responses must be provided to the whole organisation.

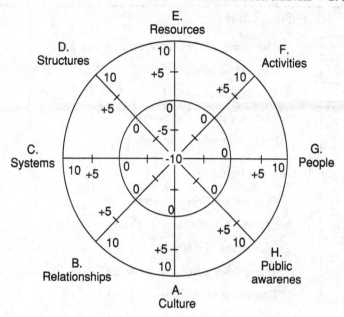

Figure 10.5. *The eight elements of a review*

Questionnaire: Instructions

This questionnaire has been designed to help us assess how effective the recent changes have been. There are 35 aspects of our organisation listed. You are asked to compare the way things are now with the way they were before the changes were introduced. Then give a score for the present situation using one of the following:

+2 = much better than it was
+1 = slightly better than it was
 0 = On balance, neither better nor worse
−1 = Slightly worse than it was
−2 = Much worse than it was

Set A. Our Culture

- [ ] The clarity of our common vision
- [ ] Our sense of mission
- [ ] The Leadership style
- [ ] The morale of the people
- [ ] Practising what we preach

Set B. Our Relationships

- [ ] Our internal relationships
- [ ] Our relationships with those we serve
- [ ] Our sense of harmony
- [ ] The quality of our team work
- [ ] The sense of 'Us' and 'Them'

Set C. Our Systems

- [ ] Our financial position
- [ ] The quality of our communications
- [ ] Your own personal growth
- [ ] Your sense of belonging
- [ ] The quality of our care for one another

Set D. Our Structures

- [ ] The balance between 'chiefs' and 'indians'
- [ ] The simplicity of our organisation structures
- [ ] The sense of liberty
- [ ] The effectiveness of committees, boards, etc
- [ ] The sharing of the work

Set E. Our Resources

- [ ] The use of your gifts and skills
- [ ] The reputation of the whole organisation
- [ ] The use of our buildings
- [ ] The use of our money
- [ ] The effective use of the full membership

Set F. Our Activities

- [ ] The quality of our activities
- [ ] The quantity of our activities
- [ ] The effectiveness of our activities
- [ ] The organisation of our activities
- [ ] The relevance of our activities

Set G. People

- [ ] People's enthusiasm
- [ ] People's commitment
- [ ] People's involvement
- [ ] People's energy levels
- [ ] People's motivation

Set H. Public Awareness

- [ ] Our visibility with the public
- [ ] Our reputation with the public
- [ ] The good will we have from the community
- [ ] Our public image
- [ ] Our contribution to society at large

The Total of scores for each set of five questions should be placed in Table 10.3. The scores from Table 10.3 can then be plotted in the Change Review Star in Figure 10.5. Join up the points to make a star, as in Figure 10.6.

Aspect of Organisation	Score
A. Culture	
B. Relationships	
C. Systems	
D. Structures	
E. Resources	
F. Activities	
G. People	
H. Public Awareness	
Overall	

Table 10.3. *Change review scores*

Interpretation

Churches, missions and organisations of all kinds are integrated in that change in one part will affect all other parts, so that a change to the structure will have its impact on relations, people, culture etc. Thus when you wish to review the effects of a change on your organisation it is necessary to consider the effects on the whole.

There will be positive and negative effects of any change. Remember that all change brings loss and all change brings stress, nevertheless, eighteen months after the change the longer term benefits should be beginning to be evident while the initial reaction to the change will have settled down – the transition will be almost complete.

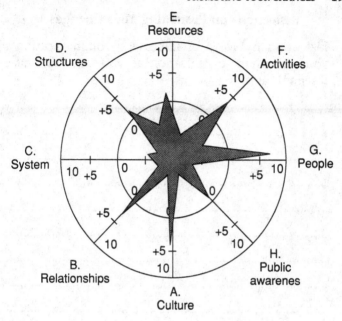

Figure 10.6. *Typical change review star*

In Table 10.3 if your overall score is positive then your change was probably worthwhile! Figure 10.6 shows the results of a review of a structure change after two years. Overall the results were positive at +28 but the organisations systems are seen to be worse than they were. In this particular case, which is quite common, the systems lagged behind the needs of the organisation.

The review provides a good opportunity to check that you are on the right course and also to identify the aspects of the organisation which need further attention.

Reflections on Promoting Your Changes

1. List as many ways of improving communication in your church or organisation as you can think of in three minutes.

    ....

    ....

    ....

    ....

    ....

    ....

    ....

    ....

    ....

    ....

2. Consider the last major change which you experienced in your church or organisation. Try to trace the four phases of transition curve through the change, see Figure 10.3.

    ....

3. What do the scores in the Change Review Star say about your organisation? What action do you need to take?

    ....

    ....

    ....

    ....

    ....

References in Chapter Ten

1. Butler, Samuel, Hudibras, quoted in *Training for Communication*, by John Adair, Gower Press, London, 1973, p. 130.
2. Eliot, George.
3. Anon.
4. Adair, John, *Training for Communication*, Gower Press, London, 1973.
5. Francis, Dave, *Unblocking Organisational Communication*, Gower Press , 1987, p. 19.
6. Exodus 14:15.

CHAPTER ELEVEN

THE ANTIDOTE TO APATHY

There is a lot of apathy about, but nobody seems to care.

Graffiti

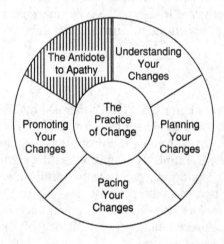

For four hundred years the Children of Israel served the Egyptians in slavery. The frightening feature of that period was that slavery had become a way of life for the Israelites. Slavery had come to be acceptable; after all, it had its good points. There was no unemployment in Egypt and work prospects were stable and long term. A job on the local building site could last for generations and the food was good – garlic and onions with roast lamb – that kind of thing. On the downside, management could be a bit heavy-handed and light-fingered, but then nothing changes much in management! Terms and conditions of employment could change without reference to the unions, but then, what's new? Family life could be uprooted from time to time as building projects moved from the lower Nile to the upper Nile, but then, as now, if you wanted work – you had to be prepared to get on your camel! Throwing the babies into the river was a bit of a trauma, but then not much different from passing them through the fire which some religions required and fewer were killed during the four hundred years in Egypt 2000 BC than are lost in one week through abortions in Europe 2000 AD!

Normal

All in all it is amazing what God's people have happily put up with and come to accept as normal over the millennia. In our times, the Church in Europe has watched over a steady decline in numbers attending[1] as the significance of the Church in national, community, family and personal life has declined over the century.

This century has also seen the fragmentation of faith in a way quite unprecedented in the history of the Church. Always subject to growth by division and multiplication, the accelerated fissioning of the Church in the second half of the twentieth century had reached the amazing level of 20 new denominations per decade in the UK alone by 1990![2] If you did not like your church you simply formed a new one. Clearly there was, and is a lot of discontent in a lot of places. Christians are not a happy lot!

Discontent

Unhappiness is a good thing when it comes to change. Discontent is necessary for action. Throughout the Scriptures we see the God of change nurturing the natural discontent in His people in order to promote change. The prophets constantly pointed to the dissatisfaction and distress in society in order to stimulate action. As we have seen in Haggai Chapter 1 the prophet puts his finger right on the spots that hurt – inflation, recession and economic stagnation – and he triggers a response.[3] In Habakkuk Chapter 1 the prophet goes as far as listing the social problems – oppression, poverty, corruption, violence and injustice,[4] while in Jeremiah, the prophet recounts the unfaithful exploits of God's chosen 'bride'.[5]

Discontent is a prerequisite of positive change. Discontent is the antidote to apathy. Discontent is a sign of life. As long as the Church remains content, complacent, self-satisfied and self-congratulating it will continue its steady decline. It will also decline if it continues to blame others for its weaknesses and calls for change in government policies and changes in society at large rather than seeking its own internal transformations. Growth, development and maturity mean change. Without change we stagnate. Like water we can become brackish, contaminated and unpalatable.

Facing up to the deep-felt discontent within the Church is not an easy or comfortable option. We fear we will not be able to cope with our deficiencies and therefore we force them underground.

In September 1990, the Presbyterian Church in Ireland met in Special General Assembly at the University of Ulster in Coleraine. This event was to celebrate the 150th anniversary of the union of Synods in 1840 and to consider the future of the Presbyterian Church in Ireland under the theme 'Transformed, not Conformed'.

During the two years of preparation for this national celebration I acted as consultant to the Conference Committee as they sought to design an event which would enable the 850 delegates to work towards the articulation of a new vision for the Presbyterian Church in Ireland. Speakers came from all over the world and, during the Assembly, study groups met to consider the implications of the issues raised by the speakers. A small production team was set up to distil the products of over 50 conference workshops and study groups.

It was a privilege and a moving experience to be present as that Special General Assembly faced up to its discontent with its witness in the divided communities of Ireland and committed itself to seek to establish a new agenda for the Church.

The product of that Assembly was called The Coleraine Declaration. It begins with the confession of the discontent. Such discontent is needed if change is to follow. The declaration goes on to describe its vision (see page 208).

Discontent is the prerequisite of change, but not simply a discontent with the way things are, but a deep discontent with the way I am.

Willingness to Change

When Moses was 40 years old he attempted to arouse a new consciousness of the need for change within God's people. He failed.[6] It was too soon. God's people were still, after 400 years of oppression, not discontent enough. Not discontent enough to accept leadership, not discontent enough to accept discipline, not discontent enough to settle their differences and move on together. So Moses had to wait another 40 years until God's people were discontent enough. 'The cry of my people comes up to me,'[7] declared the God of Jacob. After 440 years they were ready for change.

The Coleraine Declaration
The Discontent

Gathered at this great Assembly, 850 of us in all, animated and uplifted by a fresh hearing of God's word, by joyful music and by songs of praise, we have been gripped by the Assembly's theme 'Transformed not conformed'.

We confess that too often we have been conformed to this world:

- by our failure to listen to God;
- by our lack of appetite for God;
- by our failure to recognise and use the power of prayer;
- by casually assuming God's presence with us;

- by our failure to listen to one another;
- by being bound to the traditions of the past;
- by being more committed to Presbyterianism than to Christ;
- by being content with superficial fellowship;
- by our preoccupation with money and possessions;
- by our failure to enable all our members to exercise their personal ministries;
- by ministering to ourselves rather than to others;

- by our lack of concern for the divisions within the Church, the Body of Christ;
- by not challenging sectarianism;
- by being afraid to take risks for our faith.

Discontent is the prelude to changed expectations. Without discontent the old agenda will remain 'good enough', unchallenged and unchanged. It is therefore one of the roles of leadership to manage the level of discontent in

The Coleraine Declaration
The Vision

In spite of all this, we thankfully acknowledge God's mercy in calling us, unworthy as we are, to be His people, chosen and redeemed in Christ.

It is our vision that through the power of the Holy Spirit, we will be transformed, so that we may:

- be hungry for God;
- be open to his Word;
- be enriched in worship as we celebrate God's awesome and joyful presence amongst us;

- be ready to make each congregation a living example of the family of God;
- be renewed in our personal and local church life so that members contribute to the total ministry;
- be willing to adopt a simple lifestyle, no longer preoccupied with money and possessions;
- be glad to share our time, talents and money for the work of God;

- be committed to mission, not only for our own country, but in all the world;
- be responsive to the needs of the world Christ came to save;
- be present as Christ's love, Christ's justice and Christ's hope in all the world's darkness and decay;
- be concerned to proclaim with new confidence and joy the saving name of Jesus, both by word and action;
- be gifted to present Christ attractively and to apply the Word relevantly;
- be able to affirm our oneness with all who sincerely love the Lord Jesus.

God make us a joyful and expectant Church, confident in Him who has made us His people and given us a heavenly destiny.

God make us no longer a Church of yesterday but a Church of today and tomorrow.

God make us mindful of Christ's living presence in our midst, leading us where He wants us to go, no longer conformed to this world, its mind-set and lifestyle, but transformed by the Spirit's renewing power.

To God be the glory in the Church, now and for ever.

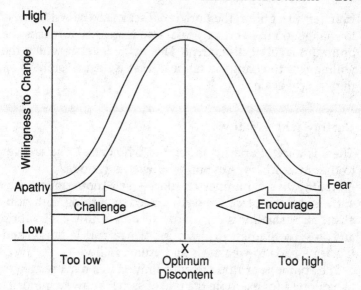

Figure 11.1. *Discontent and willingness to change*

such a way that it creates the desire and the readiness for change. But not all discontent is good.

Low levels of discontent lead to complacency and apathy. As the level of discontent rises within a community so does the willingness for change. Figure 11.1 illustrates this. It also illustrates that there is a limit to the increased willingness to change as the level of discontent rises. In other words, there is an optimum level of discontent beyond which the willingness to change begins to decline. At very high levels of discontent we find fear and hopelessness dominating and thus very little change is possible. In such situations it is not challenge that is needed, but encouragement.

The figure shows that as the level of discontent increases

from left to right on the horizontal scale, so the willingness to change, on the vertical scale, also increases. X marks the optimum level of discontent. This is the level at which the willingness to change is highest, that is, at the point Y on the vertical scale.

Dealing with Apathy

There is a lot of apathy about, but who cares? The answer to that question is 'Anyone who wishes change.'

Apathy has a number of roots – self-centredness, self-sufficiency, complacency, having need of nothing, individualism and isolationism. Apathy results in low motivation and low motivation leads to indolence and lethargy and lethargy leads to weakness and vulnerability.

The apathetic attitude may be limited to a narrow area of behaviour – for example the fate of some far away minority group being persecuted by its government, or the apathy may be an all-pervasive malaise. In Habakkuk Chapter 1 we find a high level of disregard for the plight of the disadvantaged – the poor, the widows, the orphans, etc, while in the parable of the rich farmer who had 'much wealth laid up for many years', there is a strong sense of an all-pervading indolence.[8]

The response to apathy – ours or others' – must be to arouse the motives of the apathetic. Stir them up. This can be done in six major ways. Often it is not clear which of the six options will be most successful and so you will need to experiment to see which options have the most impact on the individuals, teams or congregations. It may be necessary to use all six – and even then you will not always be successful. Change, like survival, is not guaranteed!

Behaviour Attitude Survey

Before we look at the different ways of influencing the apathetic, let us consider how you currently tend to persuade people of the need for change. On the following pages there are a number of descriptions of behaviour which can be used to influence situations and people. All are useful and appropriate in different situations, but use the questionnaire to decide which ones you tend to use more than others.

The score you assigned to each question should then be entered in the appropriate score column of the Questionnaire Score Chart, Table 11.1. Thus, your score for question

---

Questionnaire: Influencing For Change
Instructions

For each of the statements listed, please enter the number corresponding to your choice from the five possible responses given below. Enter the number:

[1] if you NEVER, or VERY RARELY do what is described in the statement.

[2] if you do what is described in the statement OCCASIONALLY, BUT INFREQUENTLY: that is, less often than most other people you see in similar situations.

[3] if you do what is described in the statement AN AVERAGE AMOUNT: that is, about as often as most other people you see in similar situations.

[4] if you do what is described in the statement FAIRLY FREQUENTLY: that is, somewhat more often than most other people you see in similar situations.

[5] if you do what is descried in the statement VERY FREQUENTLY: that is, considerably more often than most other people you observe in similar situations.

THE QUESTIONNAIRE

*When involved in situations where I am attempting to get
people to change their attitude or behaviour:*

____1.   I use moral imperatives such as 'should', 'ought',
and 'must' to persuade them

____2.   I admit my own reluctance to change

____3.   I seek help in finding solutions to problems

____4.   I communicate my belief in the value and impor-
tance of working together

____5.   I put together a good logical argument as to what
I think should be done

____6.   I let others know when they let me down

____7.   I use my authority to get things done

____8.   If others become angry or upset, I listen with
understanding

____9.   I heighten others' awareness of the benefits of
pulling together as one

____10. I put forward lots of ideas and proposals

____11. I am quick to come forward with a counter-argu-
ment if my ideas are opposed

____12. I point out mistakes in other people's ideas

____13. I verbalise standards which I think others ought
to meet

____14. I am open about my personal hopes and fears for
the change

____15. My way of speaking conveys a sense of excite-
ment to others

____16. I cause people to be more aware of the goals they
have in common

____17. I defend my own ideas for change energetically

____18. I seek assistance in important tasks

____19. I listen carefully when people express views
which are different from my own

____20. My enthusiasm is contagious

____21. My proposals have a strong impact on others

___22. I anticipate objections to my point of view and am ready with a counter-argument.

___23. I use veiled or open threats to get others to comply

___24. I acknowledge when I am uncertain or do not have the answer

___25. I summarise what others have said to make certain they have been heard

___26. I put into words the wishes of the group

___27. I will make a proposal that I feel has merit, no matter how unpopular it may be

___28. I am quick to give credit to those who work for change

___29. I express strong views about how things should be done

___30. I believe it is important to consider others' emotions and feelings

___31. I help people find common goals which strengthen their commitment to one another

___32. I draw attention to inconsistencies in others' logic

___33. I show my approval when others do what I want

___34. I let others know, directly or indirectly, exactly what I expect from them

___35. I make other people feel that they have something of value to contribute

___36. I clarify what others have said before I respond

___37. I use the language of unity to generate enthusiasm for the change

___38. I generate a feeling of 'We're in this together.'

___39. I express my ideas clearly and logically

___40. When people disagree with my ideas, I will come up with a new line of reasoning to persuade them

___41. I look for ways of kindling people's enthusiasm

___42. I talk positively about the future

___43. I encourage people to make choices

___44. I seek to strengthen people's inter-dependence

___45. I try to give control to others
___46. I build up others' self esteem
___47. I look for ways of increasing people's autonomy
___48. People feel stronger after they have been with me
___49. People come to me for advice
___50. I seek to empower people to do what they want to do
___51. I recognise when people are under pressure
___52. I encourage people to use their strengths
___53. I give positive support to those who need it
___54. I have patience with people who are afraid of change
___55. I encourage people to talk about their fears
___56. I am quick to give a helping hand if it is asked for
___57. I am prepared to alter my plans to help others cope
___58. I can spot when people are stressed
___59. People come to me when they are in trouble
___60. I encourage people in the use of their gifts.

1 goes in Column A, your scores for questions 2 and 3 go in Column B, etc. Insert a '3' for any answer which you left blank when answering the Questionnaire.

Analysing the Results

Add the numbers in each column in Table 11.1 to obtain your six scores. You will now have a total of six scores with a maximum of 50 points and a minimum of 10 points in each column. Add together all your scores and divide by six to give you your overall average.

Six basic influencing approaches are highlighted by these questions:

No.	A	No.	B	No.	C	No.	D	No.	E	No.	F
1.		2.		4.		5.		41.		51.	
6.		3.		9.		10.		42.		52.	
7.		8.		15.		11.		43.		53.	
12.		14.		16.		17.		44.		54.	
13.		18.		20.		21.		45.		55.	
23.		19.		26.		22.		46.		56.	
28.		24.		30.		27.		47.		57.	
29.		25.		31.		32.		48.		58.	
33.		35.		37.		39.		49.		59.	
34.		36.		38.		40.		50.		60	
Tot.		Tot.		Tot.		Tot.		Tot.		Tot.	

Table 11.1. *Questionnaire score chart*

A. Offering Incentives and Threats
B. Seeking Help and Assistance
C. Creating a Common Vision
D. Presenting the Rational Case
E. Developing Empowerment in Others
F. Giving Personal Encouragement

The 60 questions and the six columns in Table 11.1 have been so designed to correspond to the six approaches. Those approaches which you scored higher than the average of 30, you tend to use more. Those that you use less have a score lower than 30. Experience shows that approaches A and D have least effect when dealing with mature adults! The six approaches are described below in detail with examples from Scripture.

Approach 1. Offering Incentives and Threats
'Come, follow me . . . and I will make you fishers of men.'[9] With words like these, Jesus challenged people to move

from one life style to another. However, not every offer or incentive will have the desired effect. For example, Jesus' encounters with the rich young ruler in which the reward was eternal life resulted in a disappointing outcome for both Jesus and the young man.[10] This incident should be seen as a cautionary tale for all those who seek change. The lesson is clear – to remain independent is of greater value for some people than to be influenced. For them an influencing approach which appears to take away their choices may be seen as coercion. Coercion is an act of aggression, an act of violence and should have no place in the repertoire of Christians except in crisis situations where immediate conformity is vital for survival.

However, facing people with the consequences of remaining as they are has its place as an effective tool for change. 'Unless you repent, you shall all perish' Jesus warns his resistant listeners.[11] The consequence of failure to change can be so drastic that there is no viable option other than to paint the fearful consequences of resistance to transformation. We must change or die.

Such language with its warnings and doom-laden predictions is not popular in our world. Most people live largely without regard for the future or the longer-term consequences of their actions. 'Live now, pay later' applies to much more than the financial side of life. We may well be conscious that we will reap what we sow[12] – but it is a long time to harvest!

Offering threats or incentives is not a popular way of influencing people today, yet the Bible is full of the language of consequence and shows it to be an effective and legitimate style of influence. How much do you use it? Look back to your scores in Table 11.1. Your score in Column A indicates your tendency to use this approach. A balanced style of influence is desirable, so your score in this column should not be more than 10% above or below your average.

If it differs by more than 10% you should seek to modify your use of this style to bring it into balance.

Approach 2. Seeking Help and Assistance

'Will you give me a drink?' were the words that Jesus used to begin a radical transformation in the life of a woman from Samaria.[13] For a leader to openly seek assistance in a small change will often open the door to a closer relationship with the people and the possibilities of much more dramatic changes for the people. This willingness to be helped is the mark of true leadership and will in turn open the people to the desire to be helped to change.

To minister effectively requires us to be ministered to in return. Consider how many people ministered to Christ in the Gospels – Mary and Martha,[14] the boy with the loaves and fish,[15] Zacchaeus,[16] the Angels,[17] etc. The lesson is clear – those who seek to help others to change must first demonstrate their own need and willingness to be helped to change. This means being willing to openly share our own needs and feelings. To show our vulnerability and need for others is one of the most powerful ways of inducing change in those around. Yet my own experience shows it is often the least used of all the influencing approaches. Check your own score in Table 11.1, Column B. Do you need to use this approach much more? Go back over the questions listed in Column B. What could you do more of?

Approach 3. Creating a Common Vision

Influencing by focusing on the future rather than on the present is a very effective tool for change. Change in itself can be very threatening, so taking the mind off the transition and focusing it on the end point will often help people pay the cost of the change.

Perhaps the most widely known statements of Jesus are those found in the sermon on the mount. 'Blessed are the pure in heart, for they shall see God.'[18] These are the words of the visionary. These were the descriptions of the new Kingdom and the words excited the imagination of the listeners and caused the hearers to dream new dreams. Visionaries of the twentieth century such as Martin Luther King, Nelson Mandela, John F. Kennedy and Mikhail Gorbachev changed the world as we know it. They inspired their generations to take on new challenges by describing new futures. How did you score? Check your total in Table 11.1, Column C.

Approach 4. Presenting the Rational Case

In His teachings Jesus often used the simple power of logic to influence His listeners. 'See how the lilies of the field grow. They do not labour or spin. Yet I tell you that not even Solomon in all his splendour was dressed like one of these. If that is how God clothes the grass of the field . . . will he not much more clothe you?'[19]

There is a particular mind-set which will only give way to logic, but it is not as common as most people think. The irrational argument is actually more likely to succeed than the rational one. Our minds and our mouths are ruled by our hearts. 'For out of the overflow of the heart the mouth speaks.'[20] Check your score in Table 11.1, Column D.

Approach 5. Developing Empowerment in Others

For many people the threat of change is the threat of the loss of control. Their current position and orientation is familiar. They have little to disturb them. They have become comfortable. Their horizon is simply the edge of the rut in which they travel. To change would not be a problem provided that the pace and direction of control remained in their hands. To yield – or worse to lose control – is their greatest fear. They must remain captains of their own ships and masters of their own destinies. Such are many leaders of the world who know the meaning and power of command and want to retain it. Jesus encounters one in Matthew's Gospel. The Centurion is seeking help for his servant but is uncomfortable with the way the help is offered. 'Just say the word and my servant shall be healed.'[21] He is looking for change but needs to have it in a form which he recognises and in a form which fits with his understanding of power and authority – and Jesus is willing to respond to his needs for the 'how' of change as well as the 'what' of change.

Empowering people to change is a key task of leadership. Empowerment helps people to change in their own way, with their own success criteria rather than to have change imposed or prescribed. So ask yourself what will they do on their own? What can they be encouraged to do? What do they want to do? It is much better to enable people to realise their own change ambitions than to have them conform to your change ambitions. Look at your score in Table 11.1, Column E. How well have you done? Do you need to do more empowering?

Approach 6. Giving Personal Encouragement

The last of the approaches to influencing for change is designed to strengthen those who may have been damaged by past change experiences or simply be fearful of the change through lack of confidence. Whether it is our Lord's call to Peter to walk on the water[22] or His embracing of the blind men in their need,[23] Jesus is the Great Encourager.

Fear is the common heritage of mankind. Fear was a Genesis experience. First came shame,[24] then came fear. Things had changed and Adam was afraid.[25] To deal with the fear of change requires a delicate balance between encouragement and control. When individuals are afraid they are liable to resort to desperate and ill-considered actions at the first sign of hope. To relieve their fear people will often follow blindly the routes that can only lead to destruction.

The task facing the leader of change when the people are afraid is likely to be much longer than when the leader is faced with apathy. The senses of fear, hopelessness and frustration must be overcome one by one while still restraining the people from ill-considered, reactionary responses to the proposed change.

Let us look at how Jesus approached a disheartened group and encouraged them to regain the initiative. After His resurrection and His appearance to selected disciples, St. John recounts the first appearance of the risen Christ to the Apostles. John recalls that they were gathered in secret because they were afraid.[26] The greatest event in the history of the world had just taken place and yet it had not changed the disciples. Then, enter Jesus, centre stage. It is to be the first of many encounters which culminate in the coming of the Holy Spirit at Pentecost. Here the Church really takes the initiative,[27] but it was the result of a process of change, a process of seven steps:

1. The sharing of the news of impending change with appeals to the enthusiastic Peter,[28] the loyal Mary[29] and the disheartened Cleopas.[30]
2. The encouragement to those who are afraid.[31]
3. The call to the helpless to help others.[32]
4. A three-fold reminder of the consequences of personal commitment.[33]
5. The giving of a great commission.[34]
6. The giving of a great promise.[35]
7. The giving of a great hope.[36]

After all this they were ready to engage with the power which makes all things new! In these seven steps we see one route to encouragement, empowerment and action.

I recall such a strategy used by a Church of Scotland minister to transform a dying community. I was on holiday with my family on one of the many islands which make up the Hebrides, off the west coast of Scotland. There was only one church on the island so we went along on the first Sunday of our visit. The congregation was small and very elderly. The church was in a poor state of repair, but a new minister had recently taken over the charge. That Sunday, I recall he preached from Genesis 2:1 on the 'day of rest'. He encouraged the congregation to rest in God and to be content with what God had given. There was no challenge in his sermon other than the encouragement to trust tomorrow to God and to rest easy in Him today.

The following Sunday he preached from John 14:3 'If I go . . . I will come back,' – and he dropped the bombshell. Due to ill health he was to have a sabbatical – six months off! The reaction in the small church was obviously one of great discouragement and concern, but the atmosphere began to change as the minister went on to describe what he intended to do with part of his enforced rest. He was planning to take an extended 'holiday' to the United States of America to visit churches which had been founded and led by past members of that small island community! In addition he would visit as many of the emigrant families of the current congregation as he could in the three month trip. The buzz at the end of that service was something that I am sure had not been heard for many years in that small dying kirk.

We returned to the island a year later on the very weekend that the minister returned from his USA visit. The church was packed. It was an emotional morning! The minister gave a summary of his visit linking the little island community with churches over 10,000 strong and led by the children and grandchildren of those present.

It was to be the beginning of a great transformation in that small community. The church is now refurbished. What was a leaky, unusable church hall when we first visited the island is now a fascinating record house displaying the world-wide links of the local Christians to Christians all over the world. When I visited the island recently I had a job to find a seat on Sunday!

Actions and Reactions

Fear is a normal, healthy reaction to any dangerous situation. We fear injury, threats and accidents and act in order to minimise the risk to life and limb. Rational fear is good. It is only when fear is irrational that it must be overcome if progress is to be made.

Emotional fear causes me to imagine threats and problems in the future which have no truth in reality. I imagine the plane crashing so I won't fly. I imagine being rejected by others so I withdraw into my own world of isolated defensiveness. I imagine not having enough money to meet unexpected demands so I do not spend and become resentful of those who do. Fear is a product of my imagination. What I see is what I get. To overcome your fear change what you see. 'Open his eyes Lord that he might see Your provision,' was the prayer of the prophet when his young apprentice focused on the enemy rather than the friend.[37]

Fear of change leads to hopelessness and a sense of powerlessness. When I feel unable to influence situations or people I feel unable to influence the course of events. Then the feared-for future becomes inevitable. I can do nothing to change it. What is the use of trying? The hopelessness of the woman with the life-long haemorrhage is transformed when she hears of the power of Jesus. If only she could engage with that power.[38]

Power is the antidote to hopelessness, power which restores control, power which opens up choices, power which strengthens us,[39] power which we use together not against each other,[40] power which is already available to us.[41] And love and encouragement are the antidotes to fear.

How did you score on your ability to encourage people to change? Check your result in Table 11.1, Column E. Now set out your six scores in Table 11.2. Remembering that the average score is 30, what do you need to do more of and possibly less of?

A Threatening	B Helping	C Visioning	D Presenting	E Empowering	F Encouraging

Table 11.2. *Personal scores for influencing change*

Releasing the Antidote to Apathy

Where does your organisation, mission or church lie on the discontent/willingness to change curve shown in Figure

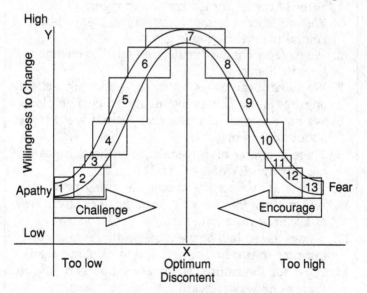

Figure 11.2. *Stages or levels of discontent regarding change*

11.1? Do the following exercise and discuss your results. What can you do to improve your position?

The statements relating to levels of discontent will help you map the level of willingness to change and the level of discontent in your organisation. Select <u>one</u> statement which best describes where you see your organisation or

---

Levels of Discontent

1. We believe that our present approach is right. We have no need to change direction.
2. We have come to realise that perhaps some things are not right in the way we operate but we are not ready to do anything yet.
3. We have committed ourselves to find out what we need to change and how to change it.
4. We see clearly what is needed but have not yet agreed how to implement any changes.
5. We are encountering a lot of problems but our commitment to action is growing.
6. We have reached agreement on what to change and how to change it.
7. We have clear goals for change and are actively engaged in implementing an agreed change plan.
8. We have started to make changes but we disagree about how to progress.
9. There is strong disagreement over the changes and we fear the risk of a split.
10. We are at an impasse, people are losing heart.
11. It is obvious that we will never make progress here, at least not for a long time.
12. Things are so bad at the moment that it takes us all our time to survive, never mind think about change.
13. I fear for the future. The organisation is dying but there is no way forward.

church at the moment in relation to change, and fit this to the curve in Figure 11.2.

Reflections on the Antidote to Apathy

1. Share your findings about levels of discontent with your group. What differences do you notice?

   ....

   ....

   ....

   ....

2. What is the influencing style most appropriate to introduce change to your situation?

   ....

3. What needs to be done now?

   ....

   ....

4. How does this release your church from apathy to change?

   ....

   ....

5. How does this release your church from fear of change?

   ....

   ....

References in Chapter Eleven

1. *UK Christian Handbook*, edited by Brierley and Longley, Marc Europe, 1993, p. 24.

2. *UK Christian Handbook*, edited by Brierley and Longley, Marc Europe, 1993, p. 24.
3. Haggai 1:12.
4. Habakkuk 1:3,4.
5. Jeremiah 2:13–32.
6. Exodus 2:15.
7. Exodus 3:7.
8. Luke 12:19.
9. Matthew 4:20.
10. Matthew 19:22.
11. Luke 13:3.
12. Galatians 6:7.
13. John 4:7.
14. Luke 16:38,39.
15. John 6:9.
16. Luke 19:5.
17. Matthew 4:11.
18. Matthew 5:8.
19. Matthew 6:28–30.
20. Matthew 13:34.
21. Luke 7:7.
22. Matthew 14:29.
23. Matthew 20:32.
24. Genesis 3:7.
25. Genesis 3:10.
26. John 20:19.
27. Acts 2:14.
28. Luke 24:34.
29. John 20:17.
30. Luke 24:31.
31. Luke 24:37–39.
32. Mark 15:11.
33. John 21:15–17.
34. Acts 1:8.
35. Acts 1:4.
36. Acts 1:11.

37. 2 Kings 6:17.
38. Luke 8:44.
39. Ephesians 3:16.
40. Ephesians 3:18.
41. Ephesians 3:20.

PART THREE

THE EXPERIENCE OF CHANGE

Change and You

Change and the Parish

The Experience of Change

Change and The Business

Change and The Diocese

Change and International Mission

Introduction

In this section of *Change Directions* I want to describe more fully the process of change within churches, missions and organisations. To do this I will use four real-life case studies in which the principles of *Change Directions* have been applied. The first case study describes the formation of a vision statement in three rural parishes under a combined charge. The second case study describes the development of a strategy for change in a diocese after the formation of the vision statement. The third case study describes the changes in the leadership practices in an international Christian mission subsequent to both the vision and strategy development which called for greater international cooperation. Finally, I describe an approach to the reorientation of a business which illustrates the principles of Change Directions, but in another guise.

These studies are 'stand-alone' chapters. Readers may study them in depth, dip into them selectively or move straight to Chapter Sixteen, Change and You.

CHAPTER TWELVE

CHANGE AND THE PARISH

As the financial pressures on churches increased and the population declined in rural areas, so the phenomenon of the 'multi-parish' increased. Research shows that a minister or ministry team may now be required to pastor as many as 15 rural parishes,[1] and this trend to multiple charges is increasing.

In some areas of the country the response has been to close the non-viable churches and combine the congregations – often against the parishioners' wishes. To close a church and merge a parish may be difficult enough in principle but often it proves impossible for the clergy to hold the two or more communities together and the net result is the loss of more than half the congregations.

Parish Records

In one diocese in the south west of England one vicar had charge of two parishes. The churches were about half a mile apart. However, the two communities would not meet together for mid-week Bible study because the two villages had been on different sides during the Civil War – almost 400 years ago! When I recounted this story to a group of clergy in East Anglia, one minister stood up and said 'I have the same in my charge. The villagers of one parish will not associate with those of the next because in the ninth century one village failed to warn the other of a raiding party of Vikings!' Parish records go back a long way!

Such was the case in Scotland in a combined charge of three parishes. The differences were historic, social and political. A vital and viable ministry to the community could have been maintained by the three parishes in cooperation, but with the three parishes declining in their isolationism, the task of the minister was enervating and depressing.

In 1991 the minister attended a *Christians in Management* course which I hold annually in Scotland. There he came across my material on vision and change much of which is now in *Change Directions*. He decided to take up the topic of vision for his own parishes as part of his forthcoming sabbatical.

We worked together on the design of his change strategy which was simple and in three stages. First, he would send a questionnaire around all the office bearers in the three parishes to find out how they actually saw the situation. Second, he would hold a vision-building event for the key leaders of the parishes, and finally, he would communicate the emerging vision through his preaching and teaching in the year following the sabbatical.

This is the record of the process. First the questionnaire is reproduced, then the Vision-Building Event is described with the emerging vision.

Gathering the Data

Questionnaires were sent out to all the church office bearers. The responses were generally positive. The questionnaire had begun to raise the awareness of the church leaders to the present and the future in relation to the community.

The questionnaire was divided into eight general topics:

A. Good points and bad points of the church
B. Satisfaction and dissatisfaction with the church
C. Development needs of the church
D. Promotion of the church in the community
E. Uniqueness of the church
F. Image of the church
G. Reputation of the church
H. Visibility of the church

The Vision-Building Event

Four weeks after the questionnaire was returned the Vision-Building Event took place. I had the challenge of leading the event since this would allow the minister to take part as a delegate. The event followed the pattern that I have developed over the last fifteen years. Although no two events are ever the same, there are some core elements in the process as we have seen in earlier chapters. This particular event took twelve hours spread over one weekend. Twenty-four delegates were involved from the combined parishes.

The Event was built around six sessions each two hours long and based on one question asked by God of His Old Testament leaders.

Questionnaire

As a church with an ongoing ministry to our changing parish, it is important that we maintain our awareness of how we are seen by others – our image – and also of how our view of ourselves – our identity – is changing over the years.

This short questionnaire has been designed to help obtain a clearer picture of how we are as a church and our vision for the future.

The answers will remain anonymous, but the minister will report a summary of the overall responses at a suitable time in his sabbatical.

A. *Good points and bad points*

If someone asked you what your church is like, what descriptions would come to your mind? These may be about atmosphere, size, age of members, activities or other issues.

Please list three good points about the church.

Now list three negative points about the church.

B. *Satisfaction and dissatisfaction*

On a more personal level, please consider your own feelings and list the three things about the church that bring you the greatest satisfaction.

Now list the three things which cause you greatest dissatisfaction.

C. *Development needs*

Please write one short key message to the church leaders about how the church should develop.

D. *The church in the community*

Imagine you are helping to put together an advert to promote the church. Jot down three phrases which you would like to use to commend the church to members and the wider community.

E. *Uniqueness of the church*

What in your opinion is unique and special about this church?

F. *Image of the church*

How do you think the church is seen by those who do not attend?

G. *Reputation of the church*

What would you like this church to be known for in five years time?

H. *Visibility of the church*

Have you any other thoughts about the church and how it is seen by the community which might help in the development of our ministry to the parish?

Session 1. Where are you? Genesis 3:8
Session 2. What is in your hand? Exodus 4:2
Session 3. What are you doing here? 1 Kings 19:9
Session 4. What do you see? Zechariah 4:2
Session 5. Can these bones live? Ezekiel 37:3
Session 6. Who will go for us? Isaiah 6:8.

Ideally these questions should be addressed over three days with time for prayer and reflection between each session. Beware! they cannot be worked through in an evening – as some churches have tried.

Session 1: Where are you?

Past	Present	Future
I see the past as dead and gone.	Small. Divided.	Good church attendance.
Healthy.	Unhappy.	Financially secure.
Wealthy.	Under threat.	Attracting more and more young people.
Happy.	Lacking commitment from many.	Free-er.
Interesting.	Stuck in rut of despair.	Surer of role/ direction.
Youthful. Large.	Traditional.	Friendly.
Institutionalised.	Distant.	Caring. Jesus.
Proud. Fuller.	Caring relationsnips.	Large. United.
More settled.	Poor attendance.	Loving. Useful.
Sure of its role.	Financially insecure.	Busy.
Warm atmosphere.	Unhappy.	More involved in national matters.
Good music.	Congregation separate. Alone.	Regain respect.
Worship.	Better music.	Promising.
God's presence felt.	Worship.	Hard road.
Dull.	God's love – felt.	Feeling secure.
Traditional.	Happy atmosphere.	Challenging.
Distant.	Musical.	Secure in God's purpose for us.
Traditional hymns.	Unattended. Sad.	Happy atmosphere and feeling of togetherness.
Respect.	Awakening.	Freedom to do what we should do.
Time being wasted.	Beginning to move.	Growing.
Standing still.	Slow to respond.	Welcoming.
	Mixed up.	Interesting.
	On the fence.	Togetherness.
	Lost respect.	Outreaching to community.
	Active.	Not being afraid.
	Full of life.	Possibilities for God's purpose.
	Energetic.	Secure togetherness.

Let us look at the outcome of each session for this rural, multiple parish.

Session 1. Where are You?

This question was the first recorded question to Adam. It is not so much a question of location as a question of status and perspective. In answering it, the person, mission, organisation or church is required to consider their past, present and future. So for this session I generally use the three-circle exercise described in Chapter Three. Each member of the leadership group was asked to draw three circles which represented their church – past, present and future. When this was done, each member was asked to write three words or short phrases to describe each of the three perspectives. These descriptions were then listed on a flip chart as shown.

Three groups of participants were formed and each group was asked to summarise one of the three columns into 'themes'. A summary of the emerging themes produced by the groups is shown in Table 12.1.

Past themes	Present themes	Future themes

Traditional
Well attended
Fellowship
	Divided views
	Mixed up
	Music
	  improving
		Growing
		  attendance
		Secure in feeling
		  and finance
		Togetherness

Table 12.1. *Emerging themes from Session 1*

The use of the 'emerging themes' technique is a very helpful way of reducing large amounts of complex data into manageable form.

Session 2. What is in Your Hand?

This question was first put to Moses as God gave him the vision of the Promised Land. Moses felt quite inadequate for the task of leadership, a not uncommon experience when a new vision emerges. However, the vision-building process works on the principle that what God calls you to do He equips you to do. Therefore an examination of what a congregation has in its hand at present will give some indication as to what the vision might call for initially. This second question produces another set of data which becomes an integral part of the vision-building process. Since vision is not about 'more of the same', but rather about fundamental change, we should not expect to see a vision emerge as a result of our answer to this question, yet its data provides essential elements to the process.

In order to carry out an examination of what a church, mission or organisation has in its hand, some kind of framework is needed. I use the one based on the review model in Chapter Ten, Figure 10.5, page 195. This enables the group to examine its strengths and weaknesses under the eight headings of culture, relationships, systems, structures, resources, activities, people and public image.

As this particular group was feeling quite vulnerable and under pressure, I asked them to focus on their strengths. This leads to encouragement and a growing belief that God is not finished yet and has already provided many gifts and resources. Table 12.2 shows the outcome of the second session for this group.

In this exhibit you will notice that the Culture and System areas are quite thin. With a little bit of prompting the Culture area can be developed. Simply ask 'What is really important to you in the way you do things here?'

Session 3. What are you doing here?

Elijah was on the receiving end of this rather uncomfortable question. He had great difficulty in answering it. In fact instead of answering the question, he twice answered another question, namely 'What have you been doing?'[2]

1. Culture	5. Resources
Involvement Cleanliness Openness to Ministry	A care-taker Notice boards Good buildings Good choir and organist Buildings Organ Christian leaders Overhead projector Video & TV Toys
2. Relationships	**6. Activities**

Good relationships with
  neighbouring churches
Good relationships with
  senior citizens
Good relationships with
  Sunday School and the
  wider church
Good general relationships
	Communion
	Prayer meeting
	Evening worship
	Bible study
	Football
	School visits regularly
	Weekly worship
	Monthly family worship
	Rainbows, Trefoil, Guides
	Old Folks' Club, Scouts

3. Systems	**7. People**

Full Kirk Session	Skilled tradesmen within
	  congregation
	Organist
	Minister
	Flower arrangers
	Visual Merchandiser
	Bankers
	Choir leaders
	A few committed Christians
	Large proportion of elderly
	  people who have time
	Small nucleus of children
	Young families who attend church
	More women attend church than
	  men

4. Structures	**8. Public Image**
Sunday School Leaders Holiday Club Session Meetings Board Meetings Fund Raising Committee Property Committee Sunday School	New people coming in Good central position Nearness to school Possibility of increased population Access to County Town Mixed housing Mixed population

Table 12.2. *Answers to Session 2: What is in your hand?*

This was much more comfortable for him since he could point back to some considerable successes.

Applying the question to the church can be done in a number of ways. Basically it requires the church to assess how it is using its time. Using the Bunting typology from Chapter 4, page 66, or some other classification such as Worship, Nurture, Fellowship and Mission allows the group to estimate the time given over to each class of activity or function. In this particular event I simply asked the group to list the activities it spent its time on. It listed the twelve shown below:

1. Spiritual guidance
2. Worshipping together
3. Building people up
4. Social relationships
5. Christian fellowship
6. Reaching out/mission
7. Supporting key life events
8. Healing
9. Teaching everybody
10. Obeying God
11. Church business
12. Service to God

These twelve were then synthesised into four areas of focus Godward, Inward, Onward and Outward and the percentage of time given to each was assessed as shown in Table 12.3.

The low outward score was to remain as a key message for the group as the new vision emerged.

Session 4. What do you see?

This question appears a number of times in the Scriptures and it is usually a prompt to look forward to what we believe God is going to do. Looking forward is not easy for many people. One way of assisting the forward-looking

Focus item	Percentage of time spent
Godward: 2 and 12	25%
Inward: 1, 2, 3, 4, 5, 8, 9 and 11	35%
Onward: 10	25%
Outward: 6, 7, 8 and 9	15%

Table 12.3. *What are you doing here?*

process is to put yourself in other people's shoes. Whose shoes? Anyone who has a stake in your future. You may not be able to describe what you think things will be like ten years from now, but, if you have children or parents still alive, what will they be wanting from you ten years from now? Most people find this a much easier question.

In the Vision-Building Event the group was asked to identify all those who had a stake or interest in the church's future. There is no priority order in the list which was produced.

Children
Kirk Session
Congregation
Minister
Parents
God
Office Bearers
Earl Haige Fund
Social Work Department
Users of Church Premises
Organist
Missionary Partners
Advertisers
Presbytery
Shelter

Clubs
Medical
School
Business
Community
The Board
Organisations
Scouts
Brownies
Police
Married
Elderly
Parents
Choir

On a recent exercise with 30 clergy, they produced over 50 stakeholders but forgot God! The next step was to apply the 80/20 rule. This rule states that eighty percent of your future success lies with twenty percent of your stakeholders. This twenty percent represents your 'Key Stakeholders' – those people or groups whose needs must be met if the church is to prosper. The group selected the seven key stakeholders shown in Table 12.4.

Key stakeholders
1. Congregation
2. Community
3. Minister
4. God
5. Children in school
6. Parents
7. Kirk Session

Table 12.4. *Key stakeholders*

Having identified the key stakeholders, the next step was to consider what these key people would be looking for 'more of' and 'less of' in the next ten years. The question is 'What will the key stakeholders expect more of and less of in ten years time?' Table 12.5 shows the responses. It is not unusual for the 'less of' column to be somewhat sparse.

The group had now answered the first three questions, but the fourth question 'What do you see?' takes more time to answer. Nevertheless you can begin to get a feel for the way their hearts and minds were moving. The elements of the vision were beginning to come together.

There are a number of ways to draw out the vision. Basically I work on the belief that God has already been speaking to the church through the Holy Spirit. What He is calling them to become is already in their hearts and

Key stakeholders	More of	Less of
Congregation	People All age worship Money, Men	
Community	Church commitment to the community Pastoral visitation Involvement in community organisations	
Minister	Support	Criticism
School children	Moral guidance Religious education School assembly Looking after the environment	
Parents	Social education Youth Club	
Kirk Session	Working out problems God's way Discipleship Making disciples	Conflict Confrontation

Table 12.5. *Key stakeholders' expectations*

minds. This means that the process must allow the group to listen to and articulate what is in their hearts. A series of prompts is usually required to draw out their thoughts. In this case the churches of the parishes were within 12 years

Session 4: What do you see by our 100th Anniversary?

1. We will be known for shining God's light in the darkness.
2. We will have more attendance, family worship, social activities, Christian leaders in key roles in the church, obeying God through discipling.
3. We will be celebrating the rebirth of the church in our area.
4. We will be bright and alive and a powerful witness to Christ whom we seek to serve in this community.
5. We will shine God's light into the darkness.
6. We will expand and celebrate.
7. We will have God's shining light.
8. By the year 2005 we will have expanded into a God-centred church secure in our love and togetherness.
9. The church and its congregation will shine out and be seen to be working in true Christian fellowship with each other and the community.
10. We will be a united congregation, spreading and teaching the Word of God in church, Sunday school and in the community.
11. We will be known as the shining light in our community, the key to Christian activities, fellowship and the rebirth of our area.
12. We will have become God's people of all ages working together so that his presence brings a new quality of life to our area.
13. The life in the heart of the community.
14. We will have a packed church from all around singing praises to God. We will be celebrating our churches' rebirth.

of their 100th anniversary and so I asked the group to complete the following sentence 'By our 100th anniversary we . . . ' They responded with the statements shown.

These fourteen responses represented the rough building blocks of the vision. Each member of the group was asked to reflect on the statements and to produce a single sentence vision which captured the essence of the fourteen initial statements. These were read out and one selected to be worked on. After some twenty minutes the group produced their first composite vision:

> By the year 2005 we will be a God-centred growing church secure in our love and togetherness.

After a time of prayer and reflection the final version was produced which shows the desire to be more active in the community:

> By the year 2005 we will be serving our communities as a God-centred, growing church, secure in our love and togetherness.

With the emerging vision articulated, the group went on to consider the thrusts for change, the mission, the goals, priorities and plans needed to begin the pursuit of the vision. These emerged in response to the remaining two sessions: 'Can these bones live?'[3] which is a test of general commitment to the vision and 'Who will go for us?'[4] which is a test of personal commitment to the vision.

The next chapter focuses on the implications of vision for a church.

References in Chapter Twelve

1. *More than one Church*, Marc Monograph Number 27, Marc Europe, 1990, p. 3.
2. 1 Kings 19:10.
3. Ezekiel 37:3.
4. Isaiah 6:8.

CHAPTER THIRTEEN

CHANGE AND THE DIOCESE

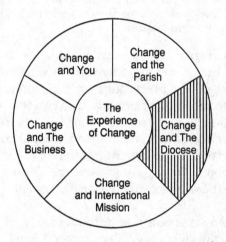

As we saw in Chapter Twelve, vision can come out of our responses to God's questions, but getting the vision is only one step. The vision must be translated into action. In this chapter I want to illustrate how one diocese moved from the creation of a vision statement produced by a very similar process to the one just described to a strategy to achieve that vision.

The Diocesan Vision

The Episcopal Diocese of Glasgow and Galloway covers the whole of the south west of Scotland from Glasgow in the Central Belt to Stranraer in the extreme south west of the country. During the first half of the 1990s, the Bishop set up a Diocesan Strategy Committee to develop a vision and strategy for change. I acted as facilitator to this committee. This is a description of their work.

The process used to articulate the vision was similar to that described in the previous chapter. The emerging vision was as follows:

> As we move towards the year 2000, God calls us, the people of the Diocese of Glasgow and Galloway to be Godward looking, Outward looking and Forward looking.

Vision statements are succinct summaries of what we believe God is calling us to become in the next period of our pilgrimage. The practicalities of the process for formulating vision mean that normally many people will not be involved directly in its formulation. Yet it is vital that all the communicants understand the vision and come to own it as their vision. Good communication of the vision is key to its adoption. The Diocesan Strategy Committee developed an expansion of the vision statement for general circulation.

This vision statement was introduced to every parish in the diocese through a specially prepared Sunday service.

What has to Change?

Since vision calls for change, the next step was to identify what the main elements of the vision would mean for the diocese. What would have to change? The Diocesan Strategy Committee examined each of the three key areas of the vision and identified the following changes.

Godward looking

Growing Godward demands a deepening of our faith and to seek:

Vision Expansion

As we move on to a new century, our Church is reaffirming its mission. The year 2000 gives an opportunity for us to measure our progress in becoming the church God calls us to be. As a Diocese we commit ourselves to act together so that by then we will know ourselves to be more:

Godward looking

As a pilgrim people led by God, growing together in worship, prayer and service we shall be equipped, relaxed and ready to respond with confidence in loving witness to the power of the Holy Spirit as we are more closely drawn to God.

Outward looking

Sharing our commitment to Christ we will work together in a common concern for each other and the world, confronting anything which diminishes human beings or diminishes God's creation. We will be an open community, accepting of one another in love and responding to the day-to-day complexity of people's lives, sharing pain and celebrating joy.

Forward looking

Building upon our rich heritage, looking forward requires us to learn and change in a spirit of hope, confident that God's power is with us to strengthen and enable us to do new things in communication with him and each other, in our worship as individuals and in fellowship together and in care and concern for God's world through mission and service as we continue to discover what it means to seek first the kingdom of God.

1. To encourage the debate on current issues and to elevate it from the secular to the Christian perspective.
2. To provide or encourage the use of counselling services for clergy, their families and lay workers.
3. To help parishes and individuals to grow in spirituality through diocesan initiatives and events.
4. To encourage spiritual growth and discernment by organising diocesan conferences/days/retreats etc on a variety of topics and where appropriate, including high powered, expert speakers or leaders. To care for carers by encouraging spiritual direction and participation in courses.
5. To encourage local churches to communicate with political parties. To include breadth of theological opinion in our approach to evangelism, worship, prayer, service and to sharpen up the Diocesan Prayer Leaflet.

Outward looking

To release people and resources in order to enable individuals and congregations to address local, national, international issues, particularly through:

1. The Social Responsibility Committee which should encourage and respond to awareness of social needs by training and enabling individuals and projects.
2. The Education Committee which should encourage training and enable people and members in faith development and skills, e.g. Sunday School, Adult Education, etc.
3. The Diocesan Missioner should encourage training and enable people and members in faith development and skills with the emphasis on mission and evangelism.
4. The appointment of a person to work alongside parishes to assist with mission audits.
5. Setting up a commission on peace, justice and integrity

of creation to provide focus and support for parish work.

6. Identifying and exploring resources in the wider Anglican Communion and other denominations.

Forward looking

To prepare structures for tomorrow which promote commitment, fellowship and forward thinking by releasing resources and by carrying out a diocesan audit which:

1. Reassesses existing structures.
2. Considers how to provide opportunities for fellowship and faith sharing.
3. Examines how to oversee the vision process and build up the importance of the Regions within the diocese.

The Diocesan Audit

As you can see, the production of a Vision Statement gives great scope for the revitalisation of existing ministries and activities. In this chapter I will focus on one major issue in particular which arose from the forward-looking theme — carrying out a Diocesan Audit, 'What did the vision mean for the way the Diocese was structured?' It was important to ensure that the diocesan structures aided the pursuit of the vision, so an audit process was designed. It was a forward-looking audit in that it examined the structures in the light of the vision rather than simply assessing their past and current effectiveness. The audit was designed to assess the structures at all levels of the church, Diocesan level, Regional level, Parish level and Clergy level. This ensured that there was an opportunity for all members of the church to be involved. The Diocese was in fact quite well structured in that it only had 18 committees. It is not uncommon for dioceses and even larger churches to support more than 50 committees!

Structures to be Assessed

The audit covered the following structures:

1. Bishop's Office
2. Synod
3. Review Committee
4. Standing Committee
5. Administration Board
6. Mission Board
7. Home Mission Committee
8. Overseas Mission Committee
9. Education Committee
10. Social Responsibility Committee
11. Cathedral Chapter
12. Bishop's Leadership Team
13. Trustees of The Diocese
14. The Regional Councils
15. The Regional Chapters
16. The Clergy Conferences
17. The Property Committee
18. The Boundaries Committee

The Audit Questionnaire

The audit was carried out through two parallel activities. The first was a series of interviews with clergy and lay leaders from across the Diocese. The second activity was the distribution of a questionnaire which was designed to reflect the elements of the vision. The questionnaire was based on the enlarged vision statement. Twenty eight aims were identified as being within the vision.

Each committee was asked four questions in relation to each of the twenty eight aims. The responses were to be rated on a scale of 0 to 10. The four questions were:

A. To what extent is this committee designed to help us fulfil the described aim of the vision?

The Aims of the Enlarged Vision Statement

Godward looking
1. To help us act/serve/respond together
2. To help us know ourselves/grow together/express our common concern for each other/fellowship together
3. To help us worship/draw close to God/pray
4. To help us equip/ready/teach/enable one another
5. To help us feel relaxed/confident in our faith.

Outward looking
6. To help us share our commitment to Christ
7. To help us express our concern for our world
8. To help us confront what diminishes creation
9. To help us be an open community/accept one another
10. To help us share pain/celebrate joy
11. To help us express loving witness
12. To help us express care/concern/mission/service.

Forward looking
13. To enable us to build on our heritage
14. To help us look forward/change/do new things
15. To encourage us in a spirit of hope/confidence in future
16. To help us to seek first the kingdom of God.

Subsidiary features
17. To help us develop our identity as Episcopalians
18. To help us develop our image as Episcopalians
19. To help us work as teams
20. To help us build our morale
21. To help us support the clergy
22. To help us develop and release gifts
23. To help us communicate internally
24. To help us communicate externally
25. To help us monitor and review progress
26. To assist spiritual growth
27. To help us promote commitment to the church
28. To help us release resources to address current issues.

B. To what extent is this committee contributing to the described aim of the vision?

C. To what extent should this committee be contributing to the described aim of the vision?

D. How easy would it be to develop this committee so that it did contribute to the fulfilment of this aim of the vision?

The people receiving the questionnaire were asked to score the committee out of 10 against these four questions which in effect looked at the *design* of the committee, its *effective contribution* to the vision, the *need for change* and finally *how easy it would be to change* the functioning of the committee to be more in line with the vision statement. Each question was laid out as shown in Table 13.1.

The table was set alongside the 28 aims of the expanded vision statement. Thus the data could be assessed at the four levels – Diocesan level, Regional level, Parish level and Clergy level.

Question	10	8	6	4	2	1	0
A. Committee design							
B. Committee's contribution							
C. Need for change							
D. Committee's ability to change							

Table 13.1. *Layout of the Audit Questionnaire for each Aim*

The Outcome at the Diocesan Level

The responses were analysed and a presentation made to the clergy and lay leadership of the Diocese. The report began with the average figures for current practice taken from the questionnaires. The maximum possible score was 100%. The overall performance of the Diocese as assessed by the members against the three key elements of the vision is shown in Table 13.2.

Godward	Outward	Forward
41%	38%	38%

Table 13.2. *Diocesan Performance Against Vision*

Godward-looking Diocese

The key to the creation of a Godward-looking church was seen as the leadership of the Bishop. Three messages were needed from the Bishop if the vision was to be realised. First, the challenge to change. The Bishop's initiative with the vision and the structural audit were seen as positive and hopeful signals throughout the Diocese. The second message must be one of example. The Bishop must ensure that the spiritual and pastoral dimensions of his ministry were fulfilled. There was a risk – a growing risk some thought – that the Bishop would become sucked into the administrative and formal functions of the role and lose sight of his 'pastoral ticket'. Clergy and lay leaders were also required to provide new models of 'faith in practice' for the people of the Diocese.

The third message that was seen to be needed was a message of confidence, that the Episcopal Church can change. Despite the many difficulties and barriers, the Bishop needed to instil a new confidence across the Diocese, based on a people with a relevant ministry and message. The Bishop must become 'focused on renewal' rather than focused on resources.

Outward-looking Diocese

The audit results showed that there were some very encouraging features in the structures of the Diocese. The Mission Board was seen to be giving a new lead and social action across the Diocese was seen as being strong and strengthening. However, there needed to be a strengthening of the identity as Episcopalians before significant improvements in this aspect of the vision could be realised.

The membership saw itself as being still very congregationalist in its thinking making each parish more independent than interdependent. This was felt to be due in part to the geographic spread of the Diocese – almost 400 square miles – but it had more to do with the history of the formation of churches many of which had been established as a result of independent local initiatives rather than as part of any coherent diocesan strategy. As Episcopalians the parishes tended to differentiate themselves, focusing on their differences in terms of churchmanship, class, wealth, etc, rather than emphasising and building on those features which they had in common.

Forward-looking Diocese

As a diocese there had been little focus on the future and there was still no strong desire to think and plan longer term. Question C, the need for change, was scored the lowest. The main concern was how to develop and sustain slow and controlled change. However it was recognised that there was a risk that the process of change could bog down, or drift slowly off course due to lack of momentum and short-term pressures.

Summary of The Diocesan Organisation

In addition to the numerical data from the questionnaires, the interviews provided an analysis based on a modification of the model described in Chapter Ten, page 195.

1. Image, Identity and Vision
2. Relationships
3. Structures and System
4. Resources
5. Commitment and Motivation

Examining each of these in turn gives a very good feel of where the Diocese was at the time of the audit.

1. Image, Identity and Vision. This was the weakest area in relation to what the Diocese wished to become. It was even more concerning when it emerged as the area in which they had least desire for change! See aims 17 and 18 of the Questionnaire, page 253.

2. Relationships. Relationships were seen to be strengthening at the diocesan level as the Boards continued to develop more cooperative relationships. There was considerable scope for improvement and a desire to see the relationships between Boards and Committees strengthened.

3. Structures and System. This was rated as a very weak area. The structures were not helping communication internally or externally to anything like a satisfactory degree. See Aims 23 and 24. Communication was always a problem. Often the failure to communicate effectively was seen to have more to do with the low interest level rather than the communication procedures.

4. Resources. The Diocese had good resources. There was a good stock of talent and although there were financial pressures in some areas, finance was not seen as a great constraint. Facilities and personnel levels were seen as adequate. Resources were being used reasonably effectively, and although there was room for improvement, it was an encouraging area. See Aims 22 and 28.

5. *Commitment and Motivation.* People were the strength of the Diocese. This was good, but it was being undermined by the lack of communication, the isolation and the differentiation.

The Outcome at the Regional Level

The Diocese has six Regions. The Regional Councils and the Regional Clergy Chapters of each Region were assessed. These structures varied very widely in performance. In some Regions they worked extremely effectively, enabling the life of the Region to be enhanced, communication to flow and influence to be exercised. However, some Regions did not function at all and perhaps worse some functioned, but very badly to the frustration of all those who participated.

It seemed that for the person in the pew, the parish church and the Synod were the major manifestations of the Diocese, for most people the Region had little or no significance. Looking at the three aspects of the vision – Godward, Outward and Forward, there was a general malfunction of the Regional structure although two appeared to have discovered formulae which were much more effective. Where there were problems, the lack of committed leadership, effective communication and a confusion of the role of the Regions contributed, to a greater or lesser extent, to a very dissatisfactory process. The Regions were certainly not, in their current mode, going to contribute much to the realisation of a Godward looking church.

In terms of the Outward aspects of the vision, there were opportunities for the churches within the Regions to do much more together. One of the reasons for the Regional structure was that geographically related churches could come together for communication, planning and activities consistent with their local needs. These opportunities had not been developed effectively. The Regions lacked an agenda. Geography still remained a barrier due to the distances involved in the south of the Diocese and the social differences still inhibited closer cooperation in the cities in the north.

The Forward view was much more positive. There was a strong desire for the Regions to get their act together and to plan and act with confidence and in concert.

The interview data provided the following analysis.

1. Regional Image, Identity and Vision.   Highly variable but generally poor with no coherent sense of vision or purpose. It was seen to be vital that the Regional structures found a way of operating which was consistent with the vision.

2. Regional Relationships.   There seemed to be little inter-regional cooperation or learning. This was not surprising given the Regional structure's weaknesses.

3. Regional Structures and Systems.   The structure itself was not seen to be the problem. It was eminently sensible to have a six-Region structure. What was missing was a coordinating body to give direction and purpose to the Regions. Although communications were criticised, it was the absence of an inspiring agenda which detracted from the validity of the structure.

4. Regional Resources.   Once again the Regions were not short of talent. There were many able and willing people who were being frustrated by the absence of a sense of direction and progress. In such situations the Region would either create its own agenda or wither.

5. *Regional Commitment and Motivation.* Given the problems with the Regions it was to be expected that for many, the Regional meetings were neither inspiring nor encouraging.

Outcome at the Parish Level

The increasing variation in church life reflected at the regional level increased in the parishes. However, there was a much stronger sense of purpose and hope at the local level than was evident at the regional and diocesan levels. This part of the Audit proved to be the most encouraging.

Looking at the three aspects of the vision – Godward, Outward and Forward at the parish level showed that the clergy tended to prefer intellect, wealth and status in the community as suitable selection criteria for lay leadership rather than spirituality!

Reaching out had more to do with social action than spiritual interaction. The Outward agenda was associated with the urban priority areas rather than with the middle class suburban wilderness. Initiatives tended to be made in response to the presence of social needs rather than spiritual needs.

Change is never easy for a church with long traditions. There was the evident temptation to resist change because 'we are rich and have need of nothing', not even change, or to resist change because 'we have had too much and can cope with no more'.

1. *Parish Image, Identity and Vision.* There was a strong sense of Episcopalians being a fringe minority in social and spiritual terms. Even within the Diocese the focus

was on difference. There was little common vision although there were plenty of individual initiatives.

2. *Parish Relationships*. There was a good sense of being together as a social group. Links to other churches were often stronger inter-denominationally than intra-denominationally.

3. *Parish Structure and Systems*. Within the parish the structures varied, but generally they were well tried and tested and functioning effectively.

4. *Parish Resources*. The smaller struggling parishes felt the lack of financial resources and the pressures were seen as being unlikely to diminish in the coming years.

5. *Parish Commitment and Motivation*. This was a highly variable aspect of parish life. It ranged from 'money is no object but my time is a different matter', to 'my time is all I have to give'.

Outcome at Clergy Level

It is always a risky business to talk about the clergy in their own house, but the Audit could not be complete without this aspect of the assessment. Looking at the three aspects of the vision – Godward, Outward and Forward – at the clergy level showed that spirituality seemed to be more of a personal pilgrimage than a community experience. Being a priest in the Diocese was a very lonely business for many. There was insufficient emphasis on being brothers and sisters together in pilgrimage for the vision to be realised. There was little expressing of common concern for each other. In this sense, the clergy were not providing the example for the laity.

Basically the clergy saw themselves as primarily

involved in a maintenance activity. Although the level of initiatives being undertaken varied widely, one common positive Outward theme was the leadership being exercised by the church in ecumenical matters. With little to encourage, and many short-term pressures, it was not surprising to find little long-term thinking by the clergy at parish level.

1. *Clergy Image, Identity and Vision.* Clergy saw themselves as having to lead, yet at the same time resenting the absence of initiatives and leadership by the laity.

2. *Clergy Relationships.* Although the relationships between the clergy and their vestries and other local leaders was good, the relationships between the clergy of the wider diocesan structures were less robust. This was evidenced by clergy attendance, or non-attendance at training events, Chapters and Councils. The clergy were not seen to be modelling team work for the flock.

3. *Clergy Structures and Systems.* Support for the clergy was not sufficient. They did not support one another effectively. Some did not want support and did not value those who might give it.

4. *Clergy Resources.* The diocesan office, although providing a good service was a long way away from parts of the Diocese since it was located on the northern edge of the Diocese.

5. *Clergy Commitment and Motivation.* It was difficult for clergy to maintain their commitment and motivation without being regularly renewed and refreshed. Given the limited opportunity for clergy to be ministered to and to minister to one another, there was a need for the clergy to

learn to demonstrate their care and concern for one another in new ways.

Recommendations

As a result of the Audit, the following seven recommendations covering the major areas for development were made.

1. The representative nature of the structure below Synod was too cumbersome. The Diocese should rely on systems for communication, not structures. It was therefore recommended that the Administration Board and Regional Councils abandon their 'representation' requirement and reduce their size.
2. Revise the remit of the Standing Committee to include the aim – 'To progress the business of Synod between Synods.' This in effect would make it an 'Executive Committee' to which all other Boards and Committees, etc, would report and be answerable. This would increase the control over the Boards and release the Synod to think forward rather then simply be a reporting forum.
3. Unscramble the Mission Board to reflect the new vision of 'Godward' and 'Outward'. Create from the Mission Board two new Boards – The Development Board which would cover the Godward aspects of the current remit, leaving The Mission Board to cover the Outward aspects of the current remit. This would strengthen the ability to pursue the vision and remove some of the overlaps which existed.
4. Create a new Regional Planning Group made up of the Bishop, the four main Board Convenors and the six Regional Convenors.
5. Streamline the Regional processes to feed and follow the Synod. Regional Councils should meet for business

three times a year – pre- and post-Synod and mid-year to review and plan.
6. All clergy should be part of a support team. Eliminate the Regional Chapters as the primary support mechanism.
7. Introduce 'regional synods' in the Regions once every three years.

Summary

The development of the new structures took two years to implement since constitutional and legal requirements had to be addressed. However the new arrangements are now in place and of course met all the turbulence that comes in the first two years of a major change.

Reflections on Change and the Diocese

1. Have we a clear vision statement?

....

....

2. Have we an expanded vision statement which helps us identify the key areas for change?

....

....

3. Have we reviewed and revised our structures in the light of the vision?

....

....

4. Which structures help us focus on the vision?

....

....

....

....

5. How could we audit our existing structures?

....

....

....

....

6. What additional support have we given to our leadership in the past two years?

....

....

....

....

CHAPTER FOURTEEN

CHANGE AND INTERNATIONAL MISSION

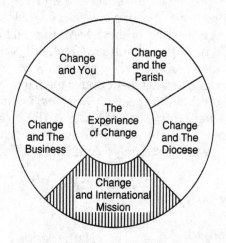

Mission Aviation Fellowship is a worldwide ministry of Christians committed to the spread of the Kingdom of God through the use of aviation and related technologies. It was founded in 1945 and by the mid 1990s had approximately 200 planes serving in 30 countries worldwide. It is the Third World's favourite airline!

Its growth in the 50s and 60s was often unplanned and unstructured as it responded to unpredictable needs and opening doors. Three separate sister organisations developed, using the same name but independently based in the UK, USA and Australia. By the end of the 1970s there were also five independent fund raising groups in Western Europe contributing to the work.

This chapter describes the way in which the Board of the UK mission was changed in response to the opportunities and challenges of a 'united' Europe. It depicts an approach to handling change within a Christian mission or business.

Inception

From 1980, representatives of those countries involved in MAF in Europe began meeting annually for fellowship and discussion. At a meeting of these MAF groups in Switzerland in April 1986, five countries – Finland, Netherlands, Norway, Sweden and the UK – agreed to work together in a flexible working arrangement under the name of Mission Aviation Fellowship Europe. Following 1986 more national MAF groups were formed and joined MAF Europe – Denmark, France, Germany and Switzerland. Each national organisation was separately constituted. Figure 14.1

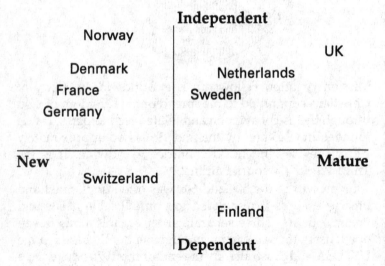

Figure 14.1. *Organisational differences: MAF Europe*

shows the spread of their maturity and independence at the beginning of the working arrangement. Some, for example Finland, began life as part of a larger national mission structure, while others, for example, Netherlands were independently constituted from their inception.

To effect a closer working relationship, in 1990 MAF UK, the largest group, placed all its existing operational activities and resources under the control and direction of a new and enlarged Board, involving the European mainland groups. By this move all MAF UK's operational activities and its support systems came under the effective authority and leadership of the new MAF Europe Board. At the time MAF UK represented over 90% of the assets, resources and personnel of the combined operation. However, this move was aimed at involving the smaller countries in the operational control of the mission. It was a bold, imaginative and generous initiative, and not without risk.

Following the restructuring of the new MAF Europe Board a number of board committees were established. These committees – Business and Finance, Personnel, Flight Safety and Domestic – had their own terms of reference, but the MAF Europe Board did not define its own remit nor the roles of its members since this needed to be done in a cooperative and evolutionary manner. This chapter describes how the new Board, made up of nine nationalities, defined its *modus operandi*.

Protocol

A number of concerns gave rise to the desire for a written Protocol for the new organisation among which were:

1. The need to clarify the purpose of MAF Europe.
2. The need to clarify the vision of MAF Europe.
3. The need to extend MAF into other European countries in a manner which enabled positive consistent growth.

Mission Aviation Fellowship Europe Purpose

1. To proclaim the love of the Lord Jesus Christ by word, work and deed, and, under God's direction, to demonstrate the concern of Christians for the spiritual, social and physical wellbeing of all people. In particular, to use our professional expertise in aviation in the extension of God's kingdom.

2. To help the people of the countries in which we fly and serve through the provision of professionally operated and safe aviation transport, logistics, communication services and the development of appropriate infrastructures.

3. To be ready to respond to the needs of relief and development work and crisis situations, working through the local church and other agencies, indigenous or international, as necessary.

4. To identify with the existing Christian Church wherever we serve, recognising our oneness with them and, so far as is possible, to support opportunities for its growth, wellbeing and expansion.

---

4. The need to clarify the relationships between MAF Europe and the other major operating MAF groups, in particular MAF US and MAF Australia.

Statement of Faith

MAF is an interdenominational mission, but in most countries it attracts people and support predominantly from the mainline, evangelical wing of the national church. To prevent protracted pseudo-theological debate it was agreed to adopt the Evangelical Mission Alliance Statement of Faith with two additional references to 'love' and 'justice'. The final version is reproduced here.

The MAF Europe Statement of Faith

As evangelical Christians, we accept the revelation of the triune God given in the scriptures of the Old and the New Testament and confess the historic faith of the Gospel therein set forth.

The sovereignty and grace of the triune God, God the Father, God the Son and God the Holy Spirit in creation, providence, revelation, redemption and final judgement.

The divine inspiration and infallibility of the Old and New Testaments as originally given and their consequent entire trustworthiness and supreme authority in all matters of faith and conduct.

The universal sinfulness and guilt of fallen man, making him subject to God's wrath and condemnation.

The substitutionary sacrifice of Jesus Christ, the incarnate Son of God, as the sole and all sufficient ground of redemption from the guilt and power of sin and its eternal consequences.

The justification of the sinner solely by the grace of God through faith in Christ who was crucified, died and raised from the dead.

The illuminating, regenerating, indwelling and sanctifying work of God the Holy Spirit.

The priesthood of all believers, who form the universal Church, the body of which Christ is the Head, which is committed by his command to proclamation of the Gospel throughout the world.

The expectation of the personal, visible return of the Lord Jesus Christ in power and glory.

The requirement of all Christians to seek justice, show mercy and in love walk humbly with God.

Purpose of MAF Europe

The second step was to agree the organisation purpose statement, see page 270. The purpose statement for MAF Europe is rather long as shown but this reflects the somewhat divergent nature of the parties concerned.

Remember that the style of the language is a reflection of the fact that nine nations and nine languages had to be accommodated!

MAF Europe Vision

MAF Europe's founder members came together in order to take advantage of existing and anticipated operational opportunities in Africa and elsewhere. The creation of MAF Europe was in line with the increasing spirit of cooperation and fellowship between many missions at that time. The emerging desire for closer cooperation reflected a number of needs, namely:

1. To bring European MAF groups closer together by the formation of a broader cultural, church and mission base.
2. To provide all European MAF groups with the opportunity for direct involvement in policy making for and

---

MAF Europe Vision Statement for the 1990s

In response to the anticipated needs,

Mission Aviation Fellowship Europe

under God's hand and through His power

will have achieved a considerable expansion

of its activities by the end of the decade,

ministering in partnerships, worldwide,

through the spiritual, personal and technical gifts

of its staff together with its national partners.

---

the leadership of operational activities in an enlarged MAF organisation.

3. To enable the MAF groups in Europe to engage in activities which they could not do as independent countries, e.g. respond to large-scale emergencies and to provide career development opportunities for staff.

4. To make more of the trends in Europe toward political and economic cooperation.

5. To increase the capacity of MAF in Europe to use its resources with optimum flexibility.

6. To benefit from the economies of size. It was recognised that the concentration of resources would lead to a strengthening of the ministry.

7. To enhance overall technical proficiency and maintenance of standards, particularly safety.

8. To acquire the benefits of multinationalism and improve the organisational interface with governments in places where MAF serves or seeks to serve.

9. To improve MAF's influence with other international sources of resource or government funding units.

The next step was to create a common vision for MAF Europe. The vision statement for the 1990s was developed by the new Board in 1991. The vision statement represents the core of the development strategy for MAF Europe.

The key words in this Vision Statement are – expansion, partnership, gifts and worldwide. These were the thrusts for change. The agenda was therefore set, the purpose and the vision had been agreed and the four main thrusts for change identified. It was time to get organised and reorganisation should start at the top.

Board Objectives

Since the backgrounds of the new Board members were very different, a basis for operation had to be agreed. What were the responsibilities of Board members? How should the Board be constituted etc? Since MAF Europe was to operate under UK Charity Law it would have to follow the Guidelines of the UK Charity Commissioners. After several extensive and animated Board discussions and a twelve-month drafting process by a special committee, it was agreed that the key Board objectives were: 'To use its corporate powers to:

1. Establish vision and agree policies.
2. Direct and resource the operations of MAF Europe.
3. Choose the Chief Executive Officer and support and guide him in his leadership of MAF Europe.
4. Ensure that, within its resources, MAF Europe meets the most need, in the safest way, at the least cost, and that this is done legally, with spiritual sensitivity, financial integrity, and in conformity with the spirit of the Protocol of MAF Europe.
5 Secure, from the MAF Europe member countries, the finances, personnel and other resources needed to fulfil the strategies and programmes of MAF Europe and meet the central costs of adminstration on the basis of the agreed budget.'

Easier said than done!

The Board's Key Tasks

Because of the nine-nation membership and the very different cultural approaches to leadership, it was also necessary to spell out the tasks of the Board. The key tasks of the MAF Europe Board were agreed to be:

1. Understand, evaluate, and approve the strategies and direction for the organisation.
2. Understand, respond to, and evaluate essential planning material produced by management.

3. Designate its members to serve on the various committees and to interact with MAF Europe management so as to augment the skills available to the organisation.
4. Organise its procedures and processes so that members can work well together.
5. Assess the eligibility for membership of member agencies and potential member agencies according to the Protocol and take action as required.
6. Take action so that appropriate skills, talents and expertise are available to support its activities.
7. Conduct the meetings of the Board with prayer and Biblical reflection as is appropriate to a Christian organisation.
8. Ensure the orderly transition of Board members, including their identification and orientation.
9. Ensure effective two-way communication between the MAF Europe Board and all participating and supporting agencies.
10. Be informed about the accomplishment of the aims of the organisation.
11. Acquire and maintain on-the-ground understanding of field conditions.
12. Ensure that the management of MAF Europe exercises good stewardship of its resources by the adoption of good personnel practices, effective systems of internal control and the regular preparation and timely submission of management information, budgets and forecasts.
13. Contribute to the strengthening and sharing of MAF Europe's Christian faith through prayer and fellowship activities.
14. Ensure that MAF Europe operates within the legal framework of the laws of the governments in whose countries we serve.
15. Devise and operate a system for evaluating the performance of the Chief Executive Officer.

16. Establish and maintain a proper plan for the succession of directors and senior managers in order to ensure continuity of leadership.
17. Review the Chief Executive Officer's evaluation of the other MAF Europe senior managers.
18. Approve appropriate international standards for public relations in MAF Europe regarding both individual and corporate statements and actions.
19. Ensure that all activities of the Board and its committees are conducted in accordance with the Protocol.
20. Provide the resources needed to fulfil the agreed strategies and plans of MAF Europe and monitor the contribution of member MAF Groups.

Such an extensive list is somewhat unusual for the Board of a Christian mission, but it helped create a common focus for the multi-cultural membership of the Board.

The Charter for the Chairman of the Board

Once again it was felt that a comprehensive 'job description' for the Board officers would be helpful.

The key objective of the Chairman is to glorify God by enabling the MAF Europe Board and its committees to accomplish their key objectives and tasks. The key tasks of the Chairman are as follows:

1. Preside at meetings of the Board and its Executive Committee.
2. Call special Board meetings as necessary.
3. Supervise the preparation of the agenda for the Board meetings.
4. Guide the Board so that it acts in the best interests of MAF Europe.
5. Establish, maintain and enhance relationships between the member countries, the Vice Chairmen, Board members and Committee Chairmen.

6. Maintain regular contact with the Chief Executive Officer of MAF Europe to support and enhance his work.

7. Participate in an advisory capacity on major organisational and programme changes.

8. Together with a Vice Chairman or other Board member, carry out, annually, an evaluation of the performance of the Chief Executive Officer.

9. Ensure the Board and Committees perform to agreed remits.

10. Ensure the Board members are given adequate exposure to MAF Europe operations and are continually updated.

11. Encourage team building among Board members.

12. Make periodic visits to the field, and ensure that there is a planned programme for such visits by other Board members.

13. Be an *ex-officio* member of all committees, and receive copies of all committee minutes.

14. Ensure orderly succession of committee members in consultation with the Vice Chairmen and the Executive Committee.

15. Confirm that the minutes of the Board Meetings properly reflect discussions as well as votes.

16. Set up, from time to time, such special assignments, investigations or studies as may be required by the Board and to monitor Board members who may be given special assignments.

17. Review with individual members, and where necessary with their MAF groups, any issues arising as a result of the deliberations of the Board and its committees.

18. Enhance and contribute to, where appropriate and possible, public awareness and public relations on behalf of MAF Europe.

19. Regularly review the performance of all individual members, Board committees and the Board as a whole.
20. Ensure that the international and inter-denominational character of MAF Europe is preserved and fostered.

The Charter for the Vice Chairmen of the Board

There were to be two Vice Chairmen required to be available to stand in for the Chairman in his absence. The Vice Chairmen should be ready and able to receive delegated tasks from the Chairman. Thus, all the requirements of the Chairman should apply to the Vice Chairmen. In addition the Vice Chairmen shall seek to:

1. In support of the Chairman, liaise with MAF groups, so that these continue to have the facility for meaningful contributions to the work of the mission and real participation in its policy setting and direction.
2. Meet with the Chairman on a regular basis for prayer and reflection.
3. Act as sounding boards for the Chairman.
4. Evaluate the Chairman's performance annually and report to the Board any recommendations for change in the way the Chairman's responsibilities are carried out or priorities revised.
5. Approve before circulation the draft minutes of the meetings over which they have presided.

The Board Members

Job descriptions are now quite common in Christian organisations, but rarely are Board members exposed to the same rigours of operation that they require of their staff. It was agreed to produce a remit for all Board members. The task proved much easier than anticipated since the UK

Charity Commissioners had done a lot of the work![1] Thus the list was relatively short. A Board member:

1. Must be spiritually mature.
2. Must have a high commitment to MAF Europe's purpose and Protocol.
3. Must have the confidence of their MAF group and be able to represent their MAF group to the Board and vote freely on all issues.
4. Should have significant cross-cultural experience and sensitivity.
5. Must be able to communicate effectively in English.
6. Must have a commitment and ability to attend Board and Committee meetings.
7. Must abide by the provisions of the Charity Commissioners.

The drafting and agreeing of these foundations of MAF Europe took over two years, but the value was not simply in the final product, but in the process of discussion, debate and negotiation. It was the process which brought the nine nations together. The resulting Protocol was only the symbol of togetherness.

Summary

Boards must give the lead in change. If the leadership cannot change, then it is unrealistic to expect the organisation to change. The Board is the custodian of the vision and must ensure that the organisation is equipped to pursue the vision. That means that the Board must first and foremost put its own house in order. This means the development of a clear remit and job descriptions for all members as well as for the officers of the Board.

Reflections on Change and International Mission

1. Has your Board, Council, Committee etc, an up-to-date remit?

   ....

2. Has each officer a written description of responsibilities?

   ....

3. Is there a written description of the expectations of all members?

   ....

4. Is there a written description of the responsibilities of all members?

   ....

5. Are the above reviewed and revised regularly?

   ....

References in Chapter Fourteen

1. *A Guide for Trustees*, The Charity Commissioners.

CHAPTER FIFTEEN

CHANGE AND THE BUSINESS

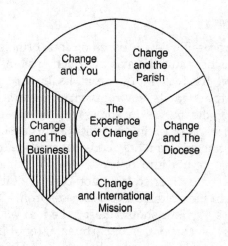

During the 1980s and 1990s many businesses underwent a process of major restructuring in response to the rapidly changing economy and business environment. One tool used by some businesses to achieve the change was a technique called 'The Core Process Review'. The Core Process Review is a systematic and participative way to review and renew businesses of any size. The terminology is self-descriptive:

The 'Core' is the heart of the business.

The 'Process' is what goes on at the heart of the business.

281

The 'Review' is a reassessment of what goes on at the heart of the business.

This chapter tells the story of the application of the Core Process Review to one business. It is presented in such a way that readers might apply the technique, or parts of it, to their own areas of responsibility whether in the world of business, mission or church.

The Principles

The Core Process Review is based on four principles. First, that any business functions as an 'open system' in which the business receives inputs from its environment and delivers outputs to its environment after processing or transforming the inputs in some way or other. Second, that over the years of its existence a business tends to become distracted from its 'core process' of efficiently transforming inputs into outputs. As a result expensive resources become diverted into 'non-core' activities. These non-core activities reduce the business profit. Third, the Core Process Review should be applied to all levels of the business – corporate, departmental and individual activities must be examined. Fourth, the Core Process Review is a management tool and therefore should be learned and applied by management rather than being applied by external consultants.

The Core Process Review is also a highly flexible tool. There is no one right way to apply it, nor is there a set period over which it should be carried out. It has been designed to be used in a wide range of settings. The Core Process Review also uses nontechnical language and is thus suitable for all types and levels of organisation.

Overview of The Core Process Review

The Core Process Review consists of six stages:

1. Creating a description of the core business purpose
2. Preparing a map of the Core Business Process
3. An identification of core and non-core activities
4. The elimination or reduction of non-core activities
5. The refocusing of the core business
6. The renegotiation of the support from inside and outside the organisation.

These stages are summarised below and described in some detail in the remainder of this chapter.

Stage One – A Description of the Core Business Purpose

'What business are we really in?' is the key question which the first stage seeks to address. On the face of it the question looks obvious, but the answer is far from clear in most businesses and it is rarely well understood by management or staff. This stage is similar to that of identifying the organisational purpose, see Chapter Four.

The object of the first stage is therefore to enable the management team to examine the nature and purpose of the business and to articulate clearly the core business purpose. This core business purpose is termed 'The Name of the Game' since the Core Process Review uses the terminology of sport as a means of communication. The Name of the Game is described in a Core Purpose Statement. This is not a Vision or Mission Statement and so the business may also wish to develop both vision and mission statements in Stage One (see Chapter Six).

The description of the Core Business Purpose can be completed at a management session of one to two days.

Stage Two – A Mapping of the Core Business Processes

Once the Name of the Game has been identified then the core business processes can be described. Here the game analogy is extended. The questions focus on how the game is played. For example, 'What is a goal in this game?', 'How do you score a goal in this game?', 'Who scores the goals?', 'Who backs up the goal scorers?', 'Who supports the game?' etc. By the end of Stage Two, a map of the core business process is prepared. This stage can be completed within a month of Stage One. Figure 15.1 shows a typical outline map.

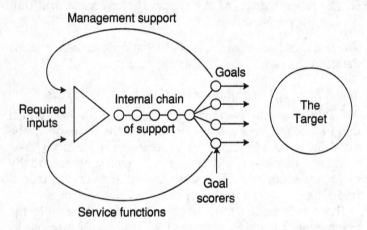

Figure 15.1. *The core process map*

Stage Three – An Identification of Core and Non-core Activities

With the core process of the business now described graphically, the present activities of the business can be examined for their level of contribution to the core process. This examination takes place at all levels of the business. Corporately and departmentally the budgets can be examined for core and non-core elements. Job content can also be assessed for core and non-core activities. This does not imply that non-core activities are of no value, management is a non-core activity in most businesses! However, the Core Process Review does imply that the business must be primarily geared to achieving the core purpose. Stage Three usually takes about three months to complete for all levels of the business.

Stage Four – The Elimination or Reduction of Non-core Activities

The streamlining of the business can now follow with a creative look at how the non-core burden can be reduced. This should be a company-wide activity and involve not only management but teams and individuals looking at their own areas of work.

All service departments, are by definition, 'non-core', yet there may be core elements in these service and management functions. For example, when managers also manage key accounts, or where the Distribution department is in direct contact with the customers, or where the Finance department is responsible for invoicing and debt collection.

Conversely, Sales – usually a core activity – may have accumulated a lot of non-core activities such as the provision of statistics, reports, meetings, travel, paperwork, etc – none of which activities actually score any goals!

This examination may take up to twelve months to complete depending on the approach and the size of the business being examined.

Stage Five – The Refocusing and Restructuring of the Core Business

As the non-core burden is identified, so the business can redirect its efforts to core activities. Internally this may mean improving the support and services to the goal scorers, while in the market place it may mean a refocusing on the customers who most meet the Core Business Purpose requirements.

The Core Process Review often results in the elimination of between 20 and 40 percent of current activity! With such a major impact on activity, it is unlikely that the current structure will be appropriate to the refocused business. A period of organisational restructuring should therefore be anticipated.

Stage Six – The Renegotiation of the Internal and External Support

Since the Core Process Review looks at the business as an open system, the final stage must be to renegotiate inputs and outputs across the organisation boundaries. These boundaries might be internal to the larger organisation or external to the suppliers and customers or the community.

Overall, the lapsed time involved in a Core Process Review is likely to be two to three years rather than two to three months.

The Core Process Review represents a major organisational development tool and is ideally suited for developing mature, sophisticated businesses and people. Such a programme of business development cannot be carried out without some training support. The training would be required in the use of the Core Process Review, but of greater importance is the training in the use of the motivational requirements of the restructured business.

I will now describe in greater detail the main elements of the Core Process Review as it was applied in one UK retail business with an annual turnover of £20 million.

The Core Business Purpose

Establishing the Core Business Purpose was the first step. With my help as the external consultant to facilitate the event this management team worked through an agenda based on the first stage of the Core Process Review. The agenda for the two days was formed around five major steps:

1. A presentation by the facilitator on the principles and practices of the Core Process Review.
2. An exploration of the Success Criteria for the business, basically, 'How do we score goals in this game?'
3. A description of the Core Business Purpose in the light of the Success Criteria.
4. The preparation of a plan to map the Core Processes and evaluate the current business's performance against the Core Business Purpose.
5. Fitting the Core Process Review into existing initiatives in order to identify the key players in the game.

The first task was to familiarise the team with the principles and practices of the Core Process Review. A presentation based on Figure 15.1 was used. The second step was to identify the business success criteria.

Business Success Criteria

What does it take to be successful in your business? How do you know you are doing 'a good job'? What does 'winning' mean in the context of your business? How do you score a goal in this game? These are the questions that the management team must first seek to answer. These are not questions to do with personal performance, but rather to do with business performance in the market place.

Any management team addressing these questions is likely to come up with a couple of dozen different criteria – all of them legitimate in terms of where the business stands at the moment. This part of the exercise will present difficulties for many missions and churches. How do you assess and measure success? Should you even try?

The management team produced the long list shown. The very wide range of criteria used by the management team is typical of most businesses. Over the years the success criteria often multiply and become unfocused.

Proposed Business Success Criteria

Profit

Customer orientation

Cost effectiveness

Quality of products and
services

Safety

Consistency of approach

Development of the
business

Long-term improvement –
not short-term only

Learning – feedback/
review

Environmental protection

Training of staff

Survival of the business

Response to competitor
attack

Standing in the market
place

Long-term growth

Maximum sustainable
profit

Development and retention
of staff

Achievement of the
planned profit
expectations

Enlargement of the
customer base

Using resources consistent
with high probability of
success

Meeting shareholders'
expectations

Defending the market
share

The same confusion can exist at lower levels of the organisation when, for example, volume is used as success criteria by sales staff when the real criterion should be profit. In a recent unfair dismissal case, a car salesman who had won the car salesman of the year award was fired because he had not made enough profit on his sales! In effect the company had two success criteria – one, 'How many cars did you sell?' and two, 'How much profit did you make?'

The next step is to strip away the less essential criteria and attempt to describe the core success criteria. The management team worked on the list to reduce it to five. The final selection is shown here.

Core Success Criteria

1. Profit
2. Customer orientation
3. Consistency
4. Development
5. Achievement of the planned
   profit expectations

The importance of the Core Success Criteria should not be underestimated. Most organisations are unsure what success actually means. What would be the core success criteria for your business, mission or church?

The Core Business Purpose

The Core Business Success Criteria also provide the basis for the Core Business Purpose. By reworking the criteria into a narrative the first description of the Core Business Purpose – the Name of the Game – will emerge. For this particular business case study it was expressed as follows:

> To develop the maximum profit potential consistently through finding, winning, keeping and developing profitable customers.

Once the first articulation has been made, the team should break for a couple of hours, preferably overnight in order to step back from the statement and come at it afresh the next day. The team revised their statement the next day to:

> To consistently achieve the planned profit objectives by finding, winning, keeping and developing profitable customers.

This is the Name of the Game. This is the Core Business Purpose. With this in place the team was able to develop an outline strategy to play this game – and win.

Winning the New Game

The Name of the Game immediately sheds light on what has to be done to win. To consistently achieve the planned profit objectives by finding, winning, keeping and developing profitable customers, means:

o Planning
o Finding
o Winning
o Keeping
o Developing
o Profitable customers

Goals and plans needed to be produced in order to reorient the business back to basics. Who is going to do what, when and how in order to reorient the business? This is a simple question which usually takes some time to answer. The management team prepared a plan as shown in Table 15.1. This enabled each member of the team to prepare their own plans consistent with the Core Business Purpose.

With the preparation of the initial action plan in response to the requirements of the Core Business Purpose and the Core Success Criteria, the way was open for Stage Two of the Core Process Review – the mapping of the Core Business Process as it existed at that time.

The Mapping of the Current Core Business Processes

Every business develops a way of doing its business which seems best to it. However, over the months and years, systems and procedures evolve which require energy to maintain and operate. Eventually the energy burden required to maintain the systems and procedures begins to outweigh their value and may even detract from the success in the game.

Table 15.2 shows the way this particular game was being

Core Business Objective	Outline Plan
The planned profit objective	1. Examine market 2. Establish desired position 3. Establish current position 4. Establish the gap 5. Plan to bridge the gap
Finding sales potential	1. Build a good data base 2. Market research 3. Prioritise customers 4. Obtain new customer lists 5. Examine new markets
Winning by providing business	1. Direction for sales team 2. Negotiation tools 3. Sales support aids 4. Improved services and products 5. Training of sales staff
Keeping profitable business	1. Keep ahead of the game 2. Look over the hill 3. Build relationships 4. Satisfy the customer's needs 5. Tie the customer in to our company
Developing markets	1. Get alongside the customer 2. Improve market intelligence 3. Show the value of our products and services 4. Make greater use of networks 5. Sell new services
Profitable Customers	1. Cull the unprofitable business 2. Know the profit targets 3. Know the cost of all activities 4. Know the cost of keeping a customer 5. Increase benefit to customers

Table 15.1. *The plan for Winning the Game*

Support roles	Back-up	Goal scorers

Management
Marketing
    department
Technical
    department
Finance
Personnel
Purchasing
Contractors
Distribution
	Sales office
	    support
	Regional sales
	    managers
		Sales staff
		Business
		    development
		    managers
		Telesales
		    representatives

Table 15.2. *Key players*

played. In the left-hand column were the people who, strictly speaking were in support roles but who were often crowding in on the game. The right-hand column shows the few people who were actually in goal-scoring positions – the key players. The centre column shows the back-up services to the goal scorers.

As has been already stated, management is a non-core activity along with all support services. What are the management contributions to the Core Business Process? Shown are the results of the team's reflections on this question.

Looking at the supporting services, the question is 'What do they need to supply more of and less of?' At this stage however it is only necessary to identify the support services for inclusion on the final Core Business Process Map. The level of complexity of the process map is a matter of choice. However, at the corporate level the level of complexity should be low.

With the completion of the Core Process Map, the team moved on to Stage Three – the identification of the Core and Non-Core activities.

Management contribution to the game

1. Meet the core players' needs
2. Information provision
3. Coaching and training
4. Setting vision and strategy
5. Setting the agenda and the priorities
6. Communicating the consistent message
7. Motivating the key players
8. Monitoring and providing feedback
9. Measuring performance
10. Providing the resources – hire/fire
11. Managing change and the boundaries
12. Giving a sense of confidence
13. Creating a climate of trust.

Core and Non-Core Activities

Activities which do not contribute directly to goal scoring are described as 'non-core'. They may be essential to the process, but, like driving to see a client or writing up reports, if the time given to them can be reduced, then it should be reduced since it takes the key player out of the goal-scoring area.

There are two basic ways to tackle the non-core activities. The first is to look at the budget and see where the money is being spent on non-core items. The second is to look at the use of time and identify the amount of effort being expended on non-core activities. The main items shown overleaf are those which the organisation members identified as being 'non-core' activities.

Refocusing

Analysing the budget in terms of core and non-core activities is simply a matter of placing an additional column on

> ## Non-core Elements of the Job
> *What has been done in the past year which has distracted you from focusing on goal scoring?*
>
> 1. Meetings to discuss the constant threat of re-organisation
> 2. Having to do own typing
> 3. Wasted opportunities
> 4. Having to spend time developing information systems
> 5. Poor journey planning
> 6. Moving from one territory to another
> 7. Incorrect information
> 8. Losing sight of the goal posts
> 9. Inability to win new business due to constant policy changes
> 10. Changes in success criteria.

the budget preparation documents to include the initial C or N as appropriate. As a guide, seek to reduce the non-core spending by 20%.

Although putting pressure on non-core budget elements and seeking to reduce the non-core activities of the key players can help improve performance, significant improvement can only be achieved through significant change. Defining the non-core activities is one thing, to agree a structure which will enable the core activities to be effectively pursued is quite a different matter. For many organisations it will mean a change of structure. This group of managers spent some time identifying the criteria for the selection of the new structure. The final list for the criteria for selection of new organisation structure was:

o Simple – with clear responsibilities
o Supports clear accountabilities

o Flat – enabling open style management
o Workable – ensuring easy interaction between management team members
o Meets the needs of the game.

Management Style

Function and structure are important, but the key to the success of any structure is the culture which is developed within the structure. Relationships had not been good in some areas of the organisation and although a new structure would help, a new style of management was going to be needed. As I have said, culture is the way we do things here, so how was this management team going to do things? The results of their discussion are shown here.

What exactly did these words mean? The Core Process,

The New Management Culture
Desired Features of the New Culture

1. Results orientated – with clear profit targets.
2. Each manager to be held accountable on the really important aspects of responsibility.
3. Open style management. This raises the question: What does 'open style' mean?
4. Quarterly reviews 'a way of life' – with major focus on how individuals can perform more effectively.
5. Senior management team (to be seen working as a team) – to direct and deal with key issues/priorities only – next levels of management to handle all other decisions.
6. The feeling that we are playing a very serious game but with plenty of enjoyment.
7. Come out as being the best.

because of its very pragmatic approach requires clear descriptions of the behaviours required for success. Most of the features required were clear enough, but what did 'Open style of management' mean? Once again the group sought to describe the core features of this concept. Their results are shown here.

Open Style Management

Consultative.
Breaking down barriers.
Having open doors.
Building confidence and trust of staff.
Being comfortable and at ease with each other.
Having no fear or favour.
All or nothing.
Having club cohesion.

These became features that the management team began to develop in a more active way over the next six months.

Final Review

A final restructuring was completed a year later and a questionnaire was used to gather the information from the sales staff on the way the business was being managed and operated in the new format. Table 15.3 shows the overall response to the questions on general performance against the purpose. Compare these with the results from the diocese in Chapter Thirteen, Table 13.2, page 255.

Finding the Profitable Business

The sales team felt that a more personalised approach to the larger customer was needed in which flexibility would be a key feature.

They wanted the new structure to lead to:

The name of the game	% performance
Finding	65
Winning	53
Keeping	80
Developing	70
Profitable Customers	65

Table 15.3. *The New Performance Levels*

o Long-term business strategies with the potential new customers
o More stability in the sales team so that relationships could be developed more effectively with the potential new customers
o Greater use of market surveys with more control of them by the sales teams
o Reduction of bureaucracy.

Winning the Profitable Business

Once again the need for flexibility was reported. More emphasis had to be placed on the benefits of the total package. More work needed to be done in promoting the quality of the company and by matching the sales approach to the customers' needs.

The new structure should therefore lead to:

o Greater consultation with the field staff on customer strategy
o Fewer mail shots and more specific package developments
o Improved manufacturer relationships.

Keeping the Profitable Business

This was one of the strongest areas but the new structure needed to be used to get closer to the customers and understand their needs and hopes for their businesses. Also the company needed to upgrade the whole quality of its service. It needed to make the company easy to deal with.

The new structure must therefore be used to:

○ Increase the level of regular contact
○ Produce right first time administration of orders, deliveries and invoices etc.
○ Create greater stability in the way the company dealt with the market place
○ Clarify policy, strategy and structure in the customer interface.

Developing the Profitable Business

Field staff needed to have access to figures which showed the profitability of any one account. They also needed to know the value to the company of each product and each deal. It was clear that most people thought that the old business was very profitable when in fact it was only just breaking even in its better years.

The new structure would ensure that the most profitable lines were promoted. This would mean targeting the expenditure more specifically. A marketing strategy was needed which would map out where and how the company intended to target the market place. Marketing activities were viewed as still very reactive and short term in nature and often did not involve sufficient sales staff input.

Summary

The Core Process Review provides excellent data for the evaluation of the development of organisations. Its flexibility makes it appropriate to any organisation wishing to systematically reassess its priorities.

Reflections on Change and the Business

The Core Process Review consists of six stages. Check your own church, mission or organisation against the six key elements of each stage as follows:

1. *A description of the Core Business Purpose.* What is your core business purpose? Refer to Chapter Four and the Reflections on page 73.

....

....

....

....

....

2. *A mapping of the Core Business Process.* How does your mission or organisation operate? Refer to Figure 15.1 on page 284 and draw a representation of your own organisation in the space on page 299.

3. *An identification of core and non-core activities.* Refer to your purpose. Make a list of the activities which directly contribute to your purpose and a list of those activities which indirectly contribute using Table 15.4. Please note that no committee – i.e. management activity – directly contributes to a business purpose.

Directly contributing	Indirectly contributing
1	1
2	2
3	3
4	4
5	5
6	6
7	7
8	8
9	9
10	10

Table 15.4.

4. *The elimination or reduction of Non-core activities.* What activities could be reduced in order to spend more time on those which directly contribute to the purpose?

....

....

....

....

....

5. *The refocusing of the Core Business.* What plans would be needed to achieve the refocusing?

....

....

....

....

....

6. *The renegotiation of the boundary support.* What new forms of support would be needed?

....

....

....

....

....

CHAPTER SIXTEEN

CHANGE AND YOU

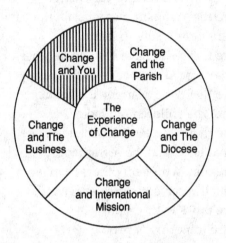

> Change is the law of life and those who look only to the past or the present are certain to miss the future.   J.F. Kennedy

How best to finish a book on change? What about a blessing, a confession, a reflection and a prayer?

A Blessing for change

Blessed are they who are nervous about changing
For they are more likely to learn.
Blessed are they who have lost out because of change
For they have good memories of the past.
Blessed are they who plan for the future
For they are the children of God.
Blessed are they who long for change
For their patience shall be rewarded.
Blessed are they who help others change
For they shall receive the greater reward.
Blessed are those with vision
For they are tomorrow's people.
Blessed are those with traditions
For their past can provide a firm base for change.
Blessed are they who suffer in transition
For God is not finished with them yet!

A Confession for change

I believe in the God of all Change.

I believe in God the Father whose eternal purposes are working change in every aspect of my life and this world. I believe in God the Son whose incarnation began a process of universal revolution which daily touches my life, renews me and transforms me.

I believe in God the Holy Spirit whose presence is the promise of change beyond my comprehension and whose power is mine to achieve the changes I am called to make and whose comfort strengthens me through whatever changes I am called to pass.

I believe in the Church as God's agent of change in this world and that as part of the Body of Christ I have a ministry of change to others. I believe that in calling me to Himself, God has called me into an eternal relationship of change.

Reflections on Change and You

In the light of your studies in Change Directions let us review your own attitudes to change in your life. Score each statement either 1 for 'tend to agree' or 0 for 'tend to disagree'.

1. I am less nervous about change now than I was.
2. I have learned from Change Directions.
3. I recognise that not all change is good.
4. Planning is a spiritual activity.
5. Change is God's way for my personal spiritual pilgrimage.
6. Everyone needs help to change.
7. Vision is necessary for life.
8. Traditions help me change with confidence.
9. Change brings stress.
10. God is in the change business.
11. God's purpose is to change me.
12. I daily experience change in my relationship to God.
13. I can face today's and tomorrow's change with confidence.
14. I believe the Church is God's agent of change in this world.
15. As part of the Body of Christ I have a ministry of change to others.
16. I share this message of change with others.
17. I support those who are burdened by change.
18. No one is beyond God's power to change.
19. God wants to change my stereotype of myself and others.
20. I welcome all I meet as pilgrims on the road of change.

If you have tended to disagree with any of the statements return to the blessing and confession, read them again, and move on to the final prayer.

A Prayer for Change

Wisdom and Love,
you call us to share
in the rebirth of Your Creation.
Through Christ
the possiblities of change become limitless
and the power to change is made available to me.
In His power may I
affirm the message of change in this world,
nurture Your people oppressed for change's sake,
discover Christ at work in dark places of this world,
receive the forgiveness
that frees me from my fear of change,
embrace those from whom I am tempted to turn away
because I think they cannot be changed,
witness to the truth that You are the God of all change,
and welcome all I meet as pilgrims
on the road of change.

So may I be ready for all the changes You give.
And may I be drawn more deeply into the transforming
fellowship of Your Holy Spirit.
Through Jesus Christ our Lord.

Amen.

INDEX